THE FUNDAMENTALS OF MUSIC COMPOSITION

LEARN MUSIC COMPOSITION STEP BY STEP

AVENTURAS DE VIAJE

WARNINGS AND DISCLAIMERS

CONTENTS

THANKS FOR YOUR PURCHASE

Did you know you can get FREE chapters of any SF Nonfiction Book you want?

https://offers.SFNonfictionBooks.com/Free-Chapters

You will also be among the first to know of FREE review copies, discount offers, bonus content, and more.

Go to:

https://offers.SFNonfictionBooks.com/Free-Chapters

Thanks again for your support.

INTRODUCTION

Welcome to the wonderland of music composition!

Let us imagine for a brief moment that you have spent months upon months learning a new instrument, you have spent hours on the internet finding the perfect bandmates, but for some reason, you forgot that you have to be able to compose your music to be able to create an EP, and now you are stuck. Well not to worry! This amazing guide will step-by-step lead you through the process of understanding music theory and how to use that knowledge to be able to compose any track from your creative mind.

In this book, you will learn the basics of music composition, as well as all the basic music theory you need to be able to compose any type of track— no matter the genre. This book and all its components will cover topics from information on music theory, sheet music reading and writing sheet music, and understanding how music composition works and how to best use all the resources on the internet and around you to compose the most amazing tracks.

The guide has been split into two sections. The first covers all you need to know when it comes to music theory. This section covers everything from beginner basics to advanced music notation and sheet music theory. The second part of the guide will cover all the information a beginner may need to start writing their compositions. It even includes the best online and software resources for both beginners and more advanced musicians and composers to consider using in their endeavors to become great writers and composers.

This process may take a while, especially if you are new to music and music composition; I know it is easy to get discouraged, even more so when you start the first time. The best way to combat that is to take breaks and do something else! There is no shame in not being able to get something right the first time— especially something as complicated as music theory and music composition. There are a lot of moving parts, but remember: practice will help you get better!

I hope that my passion for music and the musical arts are portrayed in this final installment of my music collection of guides. And whether you are a beginner or not, you find everything you are looking for.

GLOSSARY

Accent: Symbol used to indicate emphasis on a specific note.

Accompaniment: Any additional parts of an arrangement that is not considered to be the main focus that only serves as a way to support and enhance the rest of arrangement.

Adagio: The Italian word for a slow tempo indication. It is used to talk about slow movement even if faster tempo is indicated at the beginning of the arrangement.

Allegro: The Italian word used to indicate a cheerful tone, also a faster tempo. These terms are used commonly with tempo and titles of music sections.

Alto: Italian for high. Generally, males have this voice type before it breaks, or a lower female register. Generally below the soprano register.

American Standard Pitch Notation (ASPN): Used to indicate specified musical frequencies that combine a note name and an octave designation.

Bar Lines: Vertical lines that are used to create measures on a staff.

Baritone: A male voice that is considered to fall between a tenor and a bass. The tenor would be higher than a baritone, while the bass would be lower than the bass.

Bass: Commonly known to be the lower register and sonorities that can be found in music. Also refer to the bass voice for the male vocal register.

Bass (Voice): The lowest possible register for the male voice.

Beam: Horizontal lines that are used to connect notes on a stave.

Beat: A singular pulse or note being sounded and can usually be tapped along to.

Breath Mark: A symbol indicating a breath (usually for wind instruments or for vocalists) or indicating a pause (usually for percussion instruments).

Choir: Commonly known as the group of singers that will sing together at social events.

Chord: Two or more notes being played together.

Chord Loop: Chord progressions (often 4 bars) that are repeated throughout a song.

Chorus: A group of singers, singing together. Can be used as an interchangeable form for choir.

Chromatic: Refers to the notes that are not found and meant to be on the diatonic scale.

Chromatic Scale: A scale collection that consists of 12 half-steps.

Clarinet: Considered to be a woodwind instrument that is composed of a single reed.

Classical: Basic and most common word for classical music, fine music and films.

Clef: A clef is used alongside the five lines where music notation is made on. Usually indicates a specific note that sets the key signature.

Contraction: A process used to make a musical phrase shorter. Always only happens in a phrase.

Counterpoint: Can be described as the combination of two different melodic lines. The second would be considered the counterpoint for the first melodic line.

Crescendo: Italian for growing. Letting the volume grow louder.

Cycle: Cycles generally refer to a set list of songs that are performed together, as a group production.

Decrescendo: Italian for diminishing. Letting the volume become softer.

Diminuendo: Italian for diminishing.

Dot: A symbol indicating that a note value will be increased by half.

Double Sharp: Indicative of a note that has been raised by two half-steps.

Double Whole Note: Indicative that notes are split into two whole notes.

Dynamics: Loud or soft levels of sound that can be found in music and arrangements.

Falsetto: Male voice register that is used mainly for special effects. Commonly falls within the treble voice register.

Flute: Can be used to refer to various different wind instruments that are used without reeds.

Forte: Italian for loud.

Guitar: A plucked, and stringed instrument that commonly has six strings.

Half Note: Dividing a note into two quarter notes.

Half Rest: Dividing a note into two quarter rests.

Half Step: Commonly known to be the smallest interval used within Western music notation.

Harmony: The sound of two or more notes at the same time, alongside the technique used for the construction of chords into an arrangement. Commonly seen on the staves as vertical unlike notes that are written and read from left to right.

Heterophony: Textures that are linked to multiple variants on a single melodic line.

Hymn: Commonly known as songs of praise towards a saint, a hero or to a god.

Improvisation: Commonly used to make creative and different types of music when playing an arrangement.

Interval: The distance between the two pitch ranges of notes, normally counted from the lower note upwards to the higher note. The lowest note will always be the first of the interval whilst the higher one would be the final part of the interval.

Key Signature: The key signature is used to indicate the absence or presence of flat and sharp notes while also indicating naturals that are all belonging to the music arrangement itself.

Ledger Lines: Commonly known as small lines that are added on the top or the bottom of a stave to extend the staff's range.

Major: Latin for greater. Commonly used to describe the scale of notes that correspond to the Ionian mode, or the white keys on the piano (from notes C to C).

Major Scale: Commonly referred to as a collection of both whole steps(W) and half steps(H). Can be seen as: W W H W W W H.

Minor: Latin for smaller. Commonly used to describe the scale of notes that correspond to the Aeolian mode, or the white keys on the piano (from notes A to A).

Motif: The word has French origin and is defined as the theme or emotion that is used as the overarching motifs.

Natural: Commonly refers to notes that are not sharp or flat. An indicator is often added beside the note to indicate that it is a natural note.

Natural Minor: Commonly referred to as a collection of both whole steps(W) and half steps(H) that are generally ascending. Can be seen as: W H W W H W W.

Notation: Method and style of writing music. Various artists and composers have different techniques. Notation is generally done on staff paper, making the entire process easier to do as well as making the reading of notation easier.

Note: A singular sound that is represented in notation. Can only be referred to as a single tone sound.

Octave: Refers to an interval of an eight, from notes C to C or D to D.

Orchestra: From Greek origin, can be defined as a group of instrumentalists performing a cycle together.

Overture: From German origin, commonly refers to instrumental music found in opera.

Pentatonic: Commonly refers to a five-note scale, or the black keys on a piano. Can also be the white notes (C D E G and A).

Percussion: Commonly refers to instruments that are being struck to create a percussion sound.

Phrase: Commonly refers to a full musical unit that can end in a cadence.

Piano: Italian for soft. Commonly represented by a letter *p* for performers.

Pitch: Commonly refers to how low or high a sound or note is.

Polyphony: Refers to music writing in multiple parts.

Prelude: Section movement that generally comes before another, but can also refer to single pieces that are stand alone.

Quarter Note: Splits note into two-eights

Quarter Rest: Splits rest into two-eights

Quarter-tone: A tone that is commonly known to be smaller than a semitone.

Range: Commonly refers to the collection of notes that someone can comfortably sing or play on an instrument.

Rest: The length of resting periods or silence in a song.

Rhythm: One of the most essential elements that is needed to create a successful song.

Saxophone: Commonly referred to as a single-reed instrument. Most commonly used in Jazz music.

Scale: Notes that are placed in an ascending or descending sequence.

Score: Written music that can show all the notation and parts.

Section: Commonly refers to the highest division from any long musical piece.

Segment: Refers to only a part of a row.

Sharp: Sharp indicators that are added before a note to indicate a pitch raise.

Soprano: Commonly known as the highest female voice register. Commonly found with female opera singers.

Staff: Also called stave. Commonly refers to the lined paper that is used for music notation.

String: Mainly refers to instruments that use strings and create sound via vibrations with high tension.

Tempo: Italian for time. Refers to the speed at which a song or arrangement is played.

Tenor: Known as the highest male register, considered to be higher than baritone.

Texture: Commonly refers to the density as well as interaction between different voices in a song.

Theme: Similar to motif, used to create an overarching theme or feeling in a piece of music.

Time: Commonly refers to the two numbers just after the clef to indicate the metre of the song. The two numbers are considered to be the time signature.

Transposition: Used to refer to the process of moving the pitch for an interval.

Treble: Treble voice commonly known to be in the higher register. Refers to the unbroken voice of boys.

Verse: Commonly used to indicate a narrative filled section that will move the lyrical story forward.

Vibrato: A vibration technique used to cover up bad intonation.

Violin: A bowed stringed instrument that generally provides alto and soprano parts in compositions.

Voice: In music commonly refers to the indicator that a vocalist should sing a particular section.

Western: Includes European and European-colonized music.

Whole Note: Commonly divides notes into two half notes.

Whole Rest: Commonly divides rests into two half rests.

PART I

———————

MUSIC THEORY

As the title states, this section will cover the basics surrounding music theory. In this section, the guide hopes to educate you on how to read, write, and use music theory as a tool to be able to create the best possible music compositions.

This section will be split into four different chapters: each covering different basics in music theory that you will need to create compositions. While these are not rules and regulations to follow and anyone can create musical compositions, I feel that along with these basics and knowledge you can ensure to create better, more cohesive sounds.

The chapters are split into music notation basics, reading music notation basics, writing music notation skills, and reading any types of music notation.

BASIC MUSIC NOTATION

Music notation is the way music is written down to be able to read — more commonly known as sheet music. This is a clear and universally understood method of being able to read any track and play it on a set instrument. To be able to read sheet music you first need to understand the basics surrounding music notation.

Still, before you can delve deep into music notation you need to understand the basics surrounding music notes and how they are structured. This topic was briefly discussed in the Singing Lessons Book, but I will delve deeper into the information here. Music notation or music notes do not differ much when it comes to singing and playing them; knowing how to use them with regards to music notation will help your journey to music composition greatly.

There are a few things that need to be considered when you look at music notation concerning composition. Firstly, you will need a few supplies and a basic knowledge surrounding how to use those supplies. The first item that you will need is sheet music paper, preferably blank paper. It is quite easy to use and can even be drafted yourself. If however, you prefer starting the writing process in a notebook or journal before transferring over to the sheet music you are, of course, free to do so.

Notes are generally written on sheet music to keep everything organized; this helps both you and anyone who might need to read your sheet music for singing or playing purposes.

Sheet music or at least the lined paper used for sheet music creation will allow you to make notes and alterations while you are busy with the writing process.

Here there is ample space for note-taking both in the margins and between note sections.

The paper you will use, more commonly known as staff paper will look as follows:

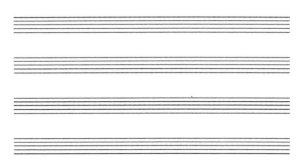

The image above shows what staff paper looks like. Staff paper is generally composed of 5 lines that are horizontally situated.

There will be ample space between lined sections and on the side margins for notes. This makes it easier to keep track of composition notes and changes throughout your writing process. On each staff, you will find both spaces and lines. Remember, sheet music or staff must be used from the bottom upwards. The next diagram will make that far easier to understand. Each staff section has 5 lines and 4 spaces.

The image above indicates the staff lines and spaces. Lines are indicated by red, and spaces are indicated by blue.

Staff sections are also split into 4 measures using bar lines. There are two different types of bar lines: regular bar lines that are used to split measures and double bar lines that are used to indicate the end of either a section or a song.

The image above indicates the different types of bars one finds in a staff. Barlines are indicated by red; measures are being indicated by blue.

Music notation is almost always written on the staff but oftentimes notes will either be higher or lower than the staff lines. These notes are often referred to as Leger Lines. You will most often just use a small horizontal line to indicate these notes, should they be higher or lower than the range in your composition.

The image above identifies and shows the three different methods and ways that ledger lines can be indicated on a staff. They can be indicated in a stepping motion as well as straight down or up, depending on how the note would rise or fall.

When you consider notes that are written on staff they are grouped into two categories: either space notes, thus written in the spaces between the lines, or line notes, thus written on the lines found within the staff. Space notes are often fully seen since they fall between the lines on the staff while the line notes will always have the line running through them.

Pitch has a very important role to play on note placement and whether or not notes would be considered high and low. This would also influence whether or not a note is a line note or a space note. Certain notes would be line notes but their pitch would be higher than a space note that would appear below it. When writing a pitch, it will always appear higher on the staff than notes that have a lower pitch.

Notes that have higher and lower pitch will be indicated in the following way.

The image above indicates different pitches and how they would differ based on placement on the staff.

The first note is generally at a higher pitch than the second, whereas the third note would be seen as a lower pitch than the fourth.

In addition to pitch, it is important to remember that certain notes can only be played within certain ranges— based on the instrument you are playing that note on. Different instruments will be able to produce different sounds and ranges. Of course, your voice is also considered to be an instrument, so it is important to note that different voices are capable of singing at different ranges.

Now that we know the basics about where you will be writing your compositions we can move on to basic notation and the notes that you will be using.

While there are more than seven notes, there are only seven key names used to indicate the notes that you will be using. Notes range from A to G, you will never find any other letter assigned to a note or its ranges. On a piano, you'll find more than the seven notes but they will be repeating as follows.

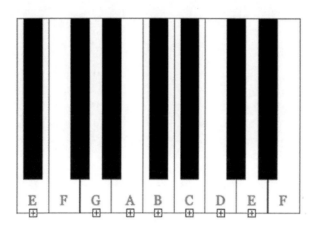

The image above shows black and white piano keys, indicating the repeating notes in red at the bottom of the keys.

Notes will always repeat— whether or not you use a piano or any other instrument. While you do get Minor and Major notes and different ranges for each note, the note itself will always be one of the notes mentioned above— ranging from A to G.

Alongside notes, you will also find something called Clef notes. These are used to indicate the key, or starting note for the section of music you are working on. Clef notes are categorized into four different types of clefs; and whilst there are four, only three of those are commonly used in music composition.

Clefs are categorized as follows:

C Clef

C clefs are not used as much anymore but can be found in music compositions that are used by viola, bassoon, and trombone players.

C clefs are somewhat confusing because it is a movable clef that changes when altered. This is not necessarily as important to know right now, as they are not commonly used at all.

Treble Clef

Treble clefs are more commonly used they are seen as the most common clefs that one can use in music notation and composition.

Treble clefs are commonly used alongside instruments that have a high pitch. Songs and compositions with pianos and piccolos generally have treble clefs included in their music notation.

1. Bass Clef

Bass clefs are exactly what you think they are. They are most commonly used alongside sounds that are more commonly low sounds.

It is important to note that most keyboard instruments will use both Bass and Treble clefs since the note range between the low and high notes is so vast.

2. Rhythm Clef

Rhythm clefs are the basic clefs that indicate the rhythm and time within a composition piece. They are often referred to as the *neutral clef;* some might also call it a *percussion clef.* The rhythm clef is mostly used by percussion players and drummers.

Basics to Remember

When you start your composition journey there is some key knowledge you will need to remember. However before we can move into composition and writing, I want to first cover some basic music guidelines and rules to always remember.

Music is an ever-growing and ever-changing field; if you add technology into the mix, the world surrounding music and composition just grows exponentially.

Music is a form of art, and any piece can be played and interpreted in thousands of different ways depending on who is reading the composition and who is playing it.

Tempo indications are a fantastic way to help those who will be playing an instrument or singing the specific composition. It is important to know what the tempo of your piece will be.

Different tempos can be used in any piece and many of these can be found in the list below:

- Largo - generally between 40 and 60 beats per minutes
- Larghetto - generally between 60 and 66 beats per minutes
- Adagio - generally between 66 and 76 beats per minutes
- Andante - generally between 76 and 108 beats per minutes
- Moderato - generally between 108 and 120 beats per minute
- Allegro - generally between 120 and 168 beats per minute
- Presto - generally between 168 and 200 beats per minute
- Prestissimo - generally between 200 and 208 beats per minute

Using any of these tempo structures will allow all those that will be using your music composition for recording or creation to do so more easily.

Along with tempo, you will also be using musical dynamics. Dynamics is used to indicate how loudly or how softly a song will be played— again aiding those using your composition to know how to do so.

There are 6 different types of common dynamics that you can use in your compositions.

- Pianissimo (pp) - considered very quiet
- Piano (p) - considered quiet
- Mezzo piano (mp) - considered a medium quiet
- Mezzo forte (mf) - considered a medium loudness

- Forte (f) - considered loud
- Fortissimo (ff) - considered very loud

Each of these dynamics has its own scale to grow louder or softer. This can be indicated by either *decrescendo* (to grow softer gradually) or *crescendo* (to grow louder gradually).

Alongside tempo and dynamics, it is essential to add emphasis and importance to specific notes. This is commonly done by adding *articulation* to the specific note. Articulation is used to indicate the *specific* note length, instead of using the note key, which will indicate the piece, general note, and breathing length.

Articulation allows those who are reading the sheet music to know how long to hold the note before moving on to the next. For example, an *accent* will indicate to a piano player how long they need to hold the key down before carrying on with the piece. Different articulations can also be used together.

Articulations are classified in the following three ways:

1. Accent - note with a lot of emphases (indicated by **<** or Λ)

2. Legato - playing the note for its full value (indicated by —)

3. Staccato - short note value (indicated by .)

There are two other types of articulations that are often used to connect notes that need to be played together.

4. Tie - multiple notes that are connected together with the same pitch (indicated by a curved line touching the notes)

5. Slur - multiple notes that are connected together with different pitches (indicated by a curved line touching the notes)

With ties and slurs, the composer will most times indicate the number of beats that this connection holds. These methods are used to connect notes so that there is no breathing space between them, or it can be used to connect notes that have been cut off by a bar line.

Repetition is a common occurrence in music; knowing how to indicate this will allow you to quickly indicate any note repetition without going through the drill of doing it again. The following diagram will indicate how repetition is shown.

The image above indicates rests and repetitions in green and time signatures in red.

The red text in block one indicates the key for the piece, while the teal icon in the fourth block indicates that the measure ahead of it will be repeated. You can also indicate how many times a section will be repeated by writing a number above the icon. Some composers use the notation : at the beginning of a section to indicate a section repetition.

Begin by truly understanding these notations. I will cover notes and how to read them in chapter 2, while note writing will be covered in chapter 3.

Technology to Help Your Journey

One of the most amazing things in this day and age are the many apps and programs you can use to make this process easier to learn. In this section, I will cover a few applications and desktop programs that will help you tremendously.

(In chapter 4 of Section 2, I will also cover any other resources that you might need along the way.)

There are hundreds if not thousands of applications that can be utilized to help you grow in whatever musical way you desire to pursue. Most app stores offer mobile versions of lessons, music reading, editing, and even entire basic versions of music studios.

The following list showcases apps that will enable you to edit, read and write your own sheet music.

Complete Music Reading Trainer

This app allows you to learn the basics of music sheet reading and writing— in the palm of your hand. The app also offers various collections that can be bought, to help you learn famous composers' pieces.

Music Crab

A musical sheet editor and creator that fits in your pocket. This app allows you to make small notes and edits on the sheet music of your choosing.

Music Tutor (Sight-reading)

This app teaches its users how to sight-read any sheet music; allows you to make any notes you need to.

Notes - Sight Reading Trainer

Similar to the app above, Notes allows you to make freehand or text notes on your sheet music whilst learning how to best utilize and learn new compositions.

forScore

forScore allows you access to a large database of music from famous composers and to create notes on them. It also allows you to export your sheet music and even share it with others.

Each of these apps hosts a variety of different types of adjustments and alterations that can be done to your sheet music. Most of these apps also allow you to import and download sheet music from famous composers, such as Beethoven.

Alterations can be made within these apps and any notes you need can be added to the sheet music itself— making it easy for you to travel with your phone or tablet, never forgetting your sheet music, or risking the paper getting lost or torn because of excessive handling.

More resources for music composition will be covered in section 2.

READING MUSIC NOTATION

One of the more important things that you as a new and aspiring composer need to know is how to read sheet music. Not only will it make writing your own compositions easier but it will provide you the knowledge and skill to read any composition no matter your skill level. Most compositions will be read from left to right, and top to bottom. However, keep in mind each composer has a different way of writing and notation.

With practice, you will be able to read notations with regards to notes and able to read notes themself. In this section, I will cover what basic notes look like and how to read any unfamiliar icons or notations that can be found in compositions.

All of the information in chapter 1 surrounding pitch, tempo, ledger lines, and dynamics will help your journey to start to read compositions and sheet music. I will be outlining the reading process in different steps to make it easier to understand and implement.

Reading Process

This process can be split into six different steps— each of them equally important. In this short section, I will cover each step and how they interlink.

Step 1: Pitch Perfect

As mentioned before the pitch is linked to how high or low a note can be. We have already discussed ledger notes and clef signs. ; now Now we can move on to the more difficult information surrounding this.

Lines and spaces are linked to the treble and bass clefs. I will only be covering those two clefs since they are the most commonly used within a composition.

Treble Clef lines use the following rhyme: **E**very **G**reat **B**and **D**eserves **F**ans

Treble Clef spaces make the following rhyme: **F**ans **A**nd **C**ooling **E**ngines

Bass Clef lines use the following rhyme: **G**reat **B**and **D**eserve **F**ans **A**lways

Bass Clef spaces make the following rhyme: **A**lways **C**all **E**veryone **G**reat

It is important to remember that notes can also be sharp notes or flat notes. When reading and writing these notes remember that the sign goes in front of the note, not after it.

Some notes can also be considered to be enharmonic sounds. This means that a sharp note can be similar to a flat note. Along with this, you can also find double sharp or double flat notes. Double sharp notes are indicated by an **x** in front of the note. This means that the specific note should be raised by 2 semitones. Double flat notes are indicated by a **bb** in front of it; like with sharp notes, the semitones need to be changed but in this instance instead of being raised, the note should be lowered.

The final pitch change that can be found with notes is the **8ve** sign that can be found above a section or specific note. This means that these notes need to be played or sung in an octave that is higher than what it was written in.

Remember, the scaling and keys that notes are written in are just as important as all the other information held within this step. Scales are like the dialect of the musical language.

Whilst there are various scales the two most important are major and minor. This means that each note has both a minor and major scale.

This means that when you are writing, you need to make sure that the notes you are writing are on the right scale. You also need to decide if it will be a major or minor scale and which note will be the defining note and scale.

In the following table, I will be giving all the relative minors for each major, as well as their respective flats (♭) or sharps (♯).

Major	Relative Minor	Sharps or Flats
C	A	None
G	E	F♯
D	B	F♯, C♯
A	F♯	F♯, C♯, G♯
E	C♯	F♯, C♯, G♯, D♯
B	G♯	F♯, C♯, G♯, D♯, A♯
F♯	D♯	F♯, C♯, G♯, D♯, A♯, E♯
C♯	A♯	F♯, C♯, G♯, D♯, A♯, E♯, B♯
F	D	B♭
B♭	G	B♭, E♭
E♭	C	B♭, E♭, A♭
A♭	F	B♭, E♭, A♭, D♭
D♭	B♭	B♭, E♭, A♭, D♭, G♭
G♭	E♭	B♭, E♭, A♭, D♭, G♭, C♭
C♭	A♭	B♭, E♭, A♭, D♭, G♭, C♭, F♭

What makes this table interesting is that each major scale has a minor scale; these two scales have the same key signature. These scales are called the Relative minor and Relative major scales— they are similar to brothers and sisters.

Key signatures play an important role in the pitch and overall sound of any composition's piece. They indicate which key the composition is written in and which notes need to be sharpened or flattened.

The indication for key signatures is done right at the start of the composition.

In the image above you can see that the key signature is indicated to be G Major or E Minor. This can be seen because of the sharp sign that is located on the F line of this specific staff.

There are different types of clefs; for this example, I used this specific clef; it can be swapped out with any of the other clefs that we have discussed previously.

Depending on where the sharp or flat indicator will be, the key will change. In the above-mentioned image, every note that is written as an F should instead be played as an F♯.

It is important to note that there can be key changes during a section in a staff. This will generally happen when you want natural notes to be played instead of sharp or flat ones. Natural notes are indicated by using the (♮) symbol.

In the above image, you can see that the red note will be played as an F sharp. The natural indicator, next to the pink notes, means that the two next notes will only be F natural notes; whilst the fourth green note will fall back into the F sharp key since there is a break in the section.

Step 2: Tempo and Groove

The beat is an equally important element in a composition. It is essential to know what the speed (or tempo) and the grouping of the said beat will be. This step allows you to gauge how fast or slow a specific section or the entire composition will be.

Most of the time the tempo and the grouping of the beat will be indicated on the stave. However, some notes may have their own tempo in a section. Universally musicians and composers use five different notations for tempo.

1. Adagio - slow tempo
2. Andante - walking tempo
3. Moderato - quick tempo
4. Allegro - fast tempo
5. Presto - fastest tempo

Tempo is commonly linked to the beats per minute in a track. Beats per minute (BPM) has become a far more popular way of indicating the tempo of a composition. Most artists and composers will indicate BPM the following way.

♩ = 120 bpm.

This example shows that the quarter note of the specific piece has a tempo of 120 beats per minute. Singular or sections of notes can have a faster or slower tempo; that is usually indicated by accel (accelerando) or rit (ritardando).

The groove or duration of the tempo works similar to how notation naming works. Similar to how we do not go beyond G, most commonly when using counting methods for beats we do not go beyond 4— and sometimes but very rarely 12. Counting in steps of four helps us keep track of the beats per minute and the overall feel of the track.

Being unable to remember the count or keeping track of what the sound is doing will make it extremely difficult to keep track of the groove or the general "feeling" that you want the track to invoke.

Time Signatures are used to indicate and explain both the tempo and groupings in a composition. They are generally indicated next to the clef of choice. Two numbers need to be read in the time signature; the top number indicates the tempo groups, while the bottom number indicates the type of beats that can be found.

The image below indicates the time signature of a simple composition. The top number indicates that each tempo will have 2 counts. The bottom indicates that the notes will be quarter notes. Common practice is to have a 4 as the bottom number; this will mean that the beat notes are considered quarter notes.

The bottom number is generally used to indicate the note that will be used for the beats. Here I will list the most common types of beat and their corresponding number.

- Whole Note (*Semibreve*) - 1
- Half Note (*Minim*) - 2
- Quarter Note (*Crotchet*) - 4
- Eight Note (*Quaver*) - 8
- Sixteenth Note (*Semiquaver*) - 16
- Thirty Second Note (*Demisemiquaver*) - 32

Step 3: Length And Duration

Note length and composition length are extremely important to know— especially note or grouping length. This step will help you recognize and understand note length.

It is important to note that there are two methods for note length that can be used. Firstly, the contemporary method uses divisions of notes, whereas the traditional method uses a naming convention. I will be explaining both in this section.

Each note will have indicators of its length. Whether or not the written symbol is filled, has a tail, or a stem will tell you the note length.

To explain the parts of a note I will show you the following diagram.

The image above is a small diagram of what a basic note is composed of. Notes differ depending on their tails, stems, and if they are filled or unfilled.

The notehead can be filled or unfilled, a note can have a stem, or not have a stem; the same can be said for a tail, some notes even have multiple tails.

You can also find beamed notes— these are two of the same notes (with tails) written next to each other.

They are simply linked by a beam instead of writing the same note twice.

I will include a small table with basic notes and their names, the contemporary name will be first followed by the traditional name will be followed in brackets.

Note Name
Whole Note (*Semibreve*)
Half Note (*Minim*)
Quarter Note (*Crotchet*)
Eight Note (*Quaver*)
Sixteenth Note (*Semiquaver*)
Thirty Second Note (*Demisemiquaver*)

These notes can be expanded on and matched with each other to get beamed notes.

The general rule for tails and stems is that if a notehead is unfilled and has no stem or tail then the note will be longer, whereas the opposite is true for a note with a stem and a tail.

Step 4: Rhythm

Rhythm is the thing that most people struggle with. It takes more than just being able to read music to be able to accurately pick up the rhythm for whatever song or composition you are working on.

The easiest way to learn how to keep track of the rhythms is to pick a piece of music and tap along with the song with your foot. Doing this over and over will allow you to train yourself by ear on how to pick up both the rhythm itself and how to keep track of the rhythm during the track.

It is important to look at the time signature when you are working on the rhythm. Knowing what the beats per bar are and what the type of beats there are will allow you to better estimate the rhythm.

When you know what the time signature is, you can do a simple math trick to find out what the rhythm will be. For example, let's say that the time signature is 2/4. This will mean that the notes are quarter notes, and there will be two beats for each note.

Alongside rhythm and tempo, you must know when there are rests and how they are indicated. Rests are used to indicate when not to play a specific note. Each note has a corresponding rest that can be used to indicate when you need not play a specific note or bar.

In the following table, I will give the note name and the rest length that it has. Most rests will be indicated before the notes, making it easier to understand when the rests need to take place.

Rest Name	Rest Length
Whole Note (*Semibreve*)	4 beats
Half Note (*Minim*)	2 beats
Quarter Note (*Crotchet*)	1 beat
Eight Note (*Quaver*)	½ beat
Sixteenth Note (*Semiquaver*)	¼ beat
Thirty Second Note (*Demisemiquaver*)	⅛ beat

Remember that multiple rests for different notes can be added into one bar, as well as for entire sections or bars— meaning that an instrument won't be played for the entire duration that has been indicated.

Whole rest *Semibreve rest*	▬	▬	1
Half rest *Minim rest*	▬	▬	1/2
Quarter rest *Crotchet rest*	𝄽	𝄽	1/4
Eighth rest *Quaver rest*	𝄾	𝄾	1/8
Sixteenth rest *Semiquaver rest*	𝄿	𝄿	1/16
Thirty-second rest *Demisemiquaver rest*	𝅀	𝅀	1/32
Sixty-fourth rest *Hemidemisemiquaver rest*	𝅁	𝅁	1/64

Step 5: Dynamics

As discussed in the previous chapter, dynamics are included to indicate how loudly or how softly a bar or section needs to be played. They play a large role in creating the desired effect or sound in a composition, so it is important to remember that whatever sound you are trying to create, dynamics will help you achieve this.

Knowing how loudly to play a certain section and bar will allow you to better understand the feeling and the emotion that the composition is trying to portray.

Dynamic indications are generally written underneath the first note of the composition and bar. Each bar can be played at different levels— so be sure to double-check the dynamic indication.

Again, the six different dynamics are as follows:

1. *pianissimo* (pp) - considered very quiet
2. *piano* (p) - considered quiet
3. *mezzo piano* (mp) - considered a medium quiet
4. *mezzo forte* (mf) - considered a medium loudness
5. *forte* (f) - considered loud
6. *fortissimo* (ff) - considered very loud

These can be used throughout the composition and even on singular notes. The best way to utilize the dynamics is to learn them; begin with making a small chart and pinning it to your wall or somewhere else to easily reference, making the process easier for yourself in the long run.

Dynamics play an important role and make sure that you are decreasing and increasing the volume at the correct intervals and sections. Having a note jump out randomly will only cause you trouble, making it more difficult to create a coherent piece.

Dynamic volume indicators allow you to indicate whether or not the volume increases or decreases gradually. This is commonly indicated by an elongated version of the < for crescendos (*Cresc*), and an elongated version of the > for diminuendo (*Dim*). If you wish you could also use the abbreviations if you prefer, making it a little easier to read.

I mentioned in Step 2 that pulse and tempo play an extremely important role in how the song will play out, so being aware of specific note emphasis will always have an impact on how the dynamics interact with your composition. Note emphasis is usually noted above the stave. There are three different methods of doing so.

1. Accent - creating sudden emphasis on notes
2. Tenuto - to lean on the specified note
3. sforzando - playing a note suddenly and with great force

These emphasizing elements are indicated in the following way:

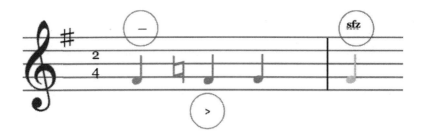

The image above is also being used to indicate the different types of dynamics that can be found within a composition. They are indicated by a red circle drawn around them. The first emphasis indicated by a - is called a Tenuto; the second, indicated by a > is called an accent; the final is called a sforzando.

Step 6: Harmony

Knowing what direction you want to take your composition in and understanding the large role that harmony plays will help both your reading and writing skills when it comes to music creation.

This final step will help you finalize the smallest details that you need to take note of before starting your journey to playing the composition. Harmony plays a large role as it helps you differentiate between which parts are meant for instruments, and which parts are for voices. When music notation first circulated t it was written purely for a single voice or instrument; whilst the music that is produced in our day and age have multiple instruments and voices — being able to find the balance between all the different elements is extremely important.

Notation will indicate that multiple notes need to be played together. This is quite a common occurrence and is something you will slowly get used to when reading music— and then when writing music.

There are two main types of music writing in the composition world: ensembles and multi-note instruments.

Ensembles are oftentimes groupings of staves for different instruments and voice bars that need to be played at the same time with different notes and their ranges. These are usually different melody lines that need to be played or sung together to create a harmonious sound.

One of the easiest ways to keep track of the section you are supposed to be playing or singing is to look at the direction of the stems. If you are playing an instrument, stems being in the correct position will allow you to keep track of your section on the stave as well as the rest of the composition.

Most composers will include additional individual parts for individual players just to make reading the staves easier.

Multi-note instruments are an important factor to take note of when you are busy reading and/or writing new compositions. Mainly because these instruments can only play one note at a time— so a separate stave needs to be written for them.

For example, common single-note instruments would be the flute, clarinet, and trumpet. Multi-note instruments are guitars, pianos, and violas.

Chords are one of the best accompaniments that one can find and use alongside a vocalist to create a wonderful harmony. This works because the vocals create the main melody, whilst the accompaniment will follow along with the vocalist to create a harmony that works with the vocals.

Knowing how to read chords is not necessary for the writing process — however, it isn't as difficult as it seems. Similar to normal notes, chords will have major and minor chords, which will be indicated by the appropriate notation.

There are hundreds of different combinations of chords that can be found. However, the four most common chords that you as a beginner will come across will be the following:

- Minor or Major chords
- Diminished or Augmented chords
- Major 7th or Minor 7th chords
- Added chords

Like any other musical notation, chords are written in a special dialect that has been created for that purpose. I will not be covering it in this book as the content on the topic can create its own book entirely. However, I will outline the three basic ways of playing chords to allow you a better understanding of the process.

Chords allow you to create a deep and meaningful sound with different instruments; knowing how to write and indicate them on sheet music will only lend to creating a fuller, more harmonious sound in the end.

Chords are played using the following three methods:

1. Block Chords

Block chords are commonly used when multiple notes are to be played all at the same time. This is a block of notes that need to be played at the same time and are usually indicated in their own stave.

2. Arpeggio

Arpeggio is a more refined manner of slowly playing all the notes in turn. What makes this a little more difficult is the fact that the notes need to be played in succession and in perfect timing with the other music to be able to fulfill its role.

3. Spread Chords

Spread chords are generally played right after each other, at a faster pace than you normally would. The pace allows for better harmonies to be created.

Step 7: Direction

The final thing that you need to keep in mind when reading and writing any composition is the direction you want the track to take. Whether it is a sad and somber sound or an energetic sound, being able to interpret sound and sheet music in the best possible way will allow you to better play and vocalize what you are reading.

A common occurrence, in older and more contemporary music, is the fact that there will inevitably be a section that repeats; oftentimes the score will change for a repeated section, — this makes playing it a little more difficult.

In this step, I will cover repetition and how it impacts your entire reading and writing process. Before we can begin I will show you how to write or read repetition on a stave.

In the image that can be seen above, the two yellow dots and the double bar lines indicate that any notes found between these two sections will be repeated. The final two dots also indicate that the player needs to go back to the start of the section, indicating that the repeat needs to happen.

In chapter 1 I covered repetition and discussed the marker that looks similar to a percentage (%) sign. This icon is used to indicate loops in the chords. Loops are repetitions of the cords that come before it, whilst the above-mentioned symbol indicates a repetition of everything that is found between the two symbols— no matter how long or short it may be.

Alongside loops and repetitions, you also have 1st and 2nd-time bars. Most beginners struggled with this, especially when they are playing the composition piece for the first time. But do not worry— though they are a bit more difficult to understand, take some time to practice and be sure to remember them as they quickly become a common occurrence in contemporary music.

1st and 2nd-time bars appear when the last bar(s) that the composer has written needs to be repeated but the ending changes upon the second playing. What will usually happen to beginners is that they play the 1st bar on the first and second playthrough, which will put them behind on timing— making the piece fall apart in terms of harmony and cohesion.

The best way to describe it is as follows:

Play the first section up until the repetition indicator, and when repeating do not play the bar (part 1) that was put right before the repetition marker, instead play whatever was indicated after the repetition marker.

I will use a diagram to make it easier to understand.

In the above diagram, you notice that the repetition marker is found at bar line number 3.

Thus, you will play bar one to three the first time, but when repeating it, you will play bar one, bar two, and bar four— skipping bar three and replacing it with bar four before moving on to the next section.

It is often missed or confused so be sure to double-check with 1st and 2nd-time bars. Also, make sure that when you are working with these bars that the 1st bar doesn't run over into the next stave.

This usually happens when the repetition indicator is located on the first bar line in the second stave. This means that the repetition would be playing bars one through four and on the second playthrough jumping from bar two to bar five.

If you struggle to comprehend this at first that is perfectly fine. It takes some time to familiarize yourself so take your time when reading through the composition and use freehand notes or perhaps a colored marker to indicate these for yourself.

The final little detail you need to know when reading and writing compositions are called stop signs. Like everything in life, there are special symbols that can be used to indicate a stop or ending to a song or composition. The most common is the double bar lines, where the second bar line is slightly thicker than the first.

More often than not, composers usually end their piece after a repetition; they indicate this by using the word *fine* (Italian for the end). This will be written alongside another note that will indicate how the piece needs to end.

A common way of ending composition pieces is using a Coda. Coda's are used to end the piece most harmoniously and satisfactorily. Coda's are also small passages that need to be played at the end of the entire piece.

These will be found at the end of your piece and usually indicated with a circular symbol that has four lines at the top, bottom, and two sides.

A composer can also opt to write *Da Capo al Coda* instead of using the symbol.

Coda   Segno

These seven steps will help your reading and writing music abilities. In the next section, I will cover how to use the knowledge you have learned in these 7 steps to writing your own sheet music.

WRITING SHEET MUSIC

In this chapter I will cover how to write sheet music. This is similar to writing your compositions, therefore I will only be outlining the process and discussing it in more detail in later chapters.

Writing sheet music is something that each composer does in their way; whilst there are basic standards that need to be followed, like indicating time signatures and keys, it is important to remember that the writing process is your own.

Find something that works and makes sense to you and slowly work into the more difficult fundamentals.

As a new composer, you already have a background in music, you have been listening to music for years so you already know how good music sounds and should sound.

Fundamentals to Remember

When writing sheet music there are a few things that you need to remember and take note of— especially when you first start out as a composer and writer. This section will cover the basics of how to start writing your sheet music and the basic formulas and notation standards.

The best way to start writing your sheet music is to set boundaries and restrictions for yourself. Being able to set an outline for what you want to achieve will help you in the long run. It will keep you from getting lost in the chaos of creation.

Having restrictions will also allow you a more structured way of getting things done— as it helps you filter out anything that isn't exactly necessary for the process of the composition.

Each piece you will be writing needs to have the following four things:

1. Tempo or beats per minute indication
2. Time signature
3. Key signature
4. Instrument List

These four elements are the most important things to help yourself structure and layout the composition piece you want to create.

In the following sections, I will give examples of what you can use for each element. Let's consider that we want to write a piece for a stringed instrument, like a violin or a viola.

Tempo

The tempo of your piece will be the base of how fast or slow you want the piece to be. It indicates the beats per minute and will help your instruments harmonize together with your vocals.

- 30 beats per minute will mean that there is one beat every two seconds.
- 60 beats per minute will mean that there is one beat for every second in the track.
- 120 beats per minute mean that there are two beats for every second in the track.

That is the easiest way to split your beats and tempo, allowing you to keep track of the pulse during the composition and playing stage.

Time Signature

Time signatures will help both you and anyone who wants to play or record your music. The time signature will allow them to keep track of the tempo and the amount of notes that need to be inside that designated tempo bracket.

For the sake of the example, we will use the common time signature of 4/4.

Key Signature

The key signature indicates the main key for the composition. This will be the starting key; you will move forward with notes and their notation from there. The key signature also allows you to indicate the minor or major that will occur within the composition.

For this example, we will be using a C Major key signature.

Instrument List

Sitting down and making a list of the instruments that you want the piece to have will allow you to allocate all the different tempos and style changes that you want to happen in the song. As a beginner, I suggest beginning with one instrument and finishing that section before moving on to another.

For our example, we will use a violin as our main instrument.

The basic outline of what we just discussed and how it will be portrayed will look as follows. It is important to note that the tempo (or beats per minute) will not always be indicated by the composer.

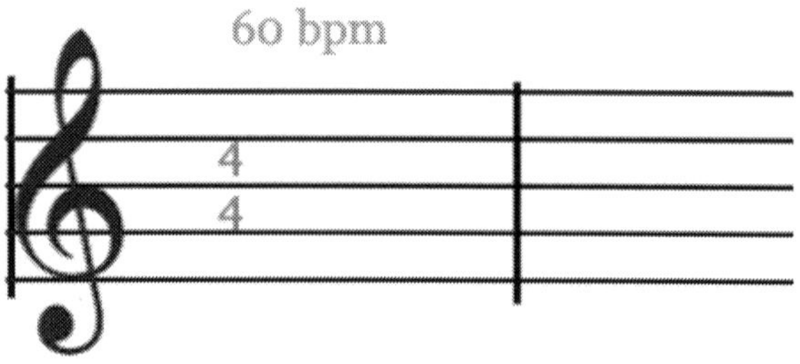

When you first start you can simply use lined paper for your basic notes, but I suggest finding staff paper online and printing it to make things easier for yourself. You can also buy a notebook that is created specifically for composition and will help you in the long run as it will allow you to take better notes.

Always be patient and take your time when you are going through the composition process. Start with a single note, for a single instrument and imagine what it would sound like— take your time to slowly imagine what the sound will evolve into, and then move forward with your vision.

There are three things that you need to focus on when you are starting to write your sheet music. They are the fundamentals that every single composition piece has to make it successful. These three things are:

1. Melody

Melody is the most difficult part of a composition. It is often just a single line of notes that need to be blended and adapted to make the entire track come together.

2. Form

The way that the beginning, middle, and end of the track are pieced together will allow you to portray and evoke the feelings you want to evoke in others through music.

3. Harmony

Harmony is the special, somewhat magical tool that blends every note and line together to bring the masterpiece you have created to life.

Knowing and focusing on these three things will help your composition piece be more detailed and filled with more emotion and feeling than just slapping some instruments together and hoping for the best.

You are obviously writing your own music because you want to share an experience— you want to share your vision and dreams with people. Music is one of the most powerful and unique ways to share these inner experiences with others.

The most important thing to remember during this entire process is that you are just a beginner— you need to give yourself some slack. You won't be as good as Beethoven or Mozart the first time you sit down to write your composition, so take your time and enjoy the process.

Of course, the process might be tough and you might struggle every now and then but that is part of learning.

Tools Of the Trade

There are a bunch of lists I can whip out and endless rhymes I can teach you, but unless you have the right tools for the job all of that will be useless to you.

I want to let you know that while these are the items I think you need to be successful in your composition endeavors various other substitutes can be used. I have added many alternatives here, but with your own research, you may be able to branch out further.

Whilst not all of these are physical items, they are all needed to help you succeed at this task. There are five things I deem essential for every new composer.

Composition Area of Focus:

1. *Ambient Sound*

One of the most important things to remember is that when you are composing and recording new music you don't want there to be random fan sounds or dripping taps distracting you from what you are doing.

The best way to avoid ambient sound is to switch off anything in your immediate vicinity that can make a sound. If you can, perhaps consider adding some thin insulation inside the room you work in to be able to block out some sounds. If this is not an option try and find a spot in the house where it is quietest to work.

2. *Privacy*

Privacy goes hand in hand with ambient sound. You must find a spot where you will be able to work undisturbed for however long you want to focus.

Having family members or animals constantly barge in and bother you might become a problem later on, so try and find a space with a door that you can lock for the duration of the time you spend composing. Remember that oftentimes you won't compose for just ten minutes and be done with it— you might spend three or four hours focused on just one bar of composition! Therefore having a private and comfortable space where you can do so will undoubtedly only help you.

3. *Feng Shui*

Not a lot of people focus on the space they do occupy and assume that having a small cluttered space will be fine, but I have found that having a space that you find aesthetically pleasing will help both your inspiration and overall comfort level when you are busy composing.

Make sure that you keep your notes and desk organized when you are not working on your composition. Take a few minutes before and after every session to simply organize your space. You can also add some inspiration posters or albums from artists you admire— make the space your own and let your creative juices flow.

4. *Capabilities*

Your capabilities and the tools you need while you are composing play a big role in how successful the outcome will be. It is important to have all of your necessary items with you, making it easier to work in privacy and peace.

Having your printer in a different room will keep you from focusing as printing new music or notes will break your concentration because you have to get up and leave the space.

I deem the following items as necessary in your space:

- **Writing Materials**

Having enough pens and pencils, as well as any other form of writing equipment will allow you to focus on the task at hand without having to rifle through your desk for 30 minutes on the hunt for a pencil.

I opt for working on a computer when doing composition, but if you enjoy old school methods before moving everything over to a digital form I suggest using a pencil. This enables you to erase any mistakes or changes you want to make.

Oftentimes I will start a draft composition on paper, and plan it out, taking my time to make as many notes as possible. I spend time making sure the notes and composition are exactly how I want them to be before moving to my digital platform.

- **Printer**

I mainly use my printer for the final draft. It is also used when I'm printing clean staff paper or a reference composition. My printer is in the back of my room, out of the way, but not far enough for me to have to walk around to get to it, making the overall workflow of printing sheet music and final drafts far easier.

- **Computer**

As mentioned before I work on both a digital platform as well as on paper. Having access to both of these at the same time makes things much easier for me. Especially if I have notes or commentary on my computer that I have to double-check, — as well as the other way around.

I love transferring my notes to a digital version to make it easier to keep track of since I can just save it in the online cloud storage and have access to it on the go. Many software even allows you to edit and make changes to the composition on the go, especially if they have a mobile version of their app available.

I personally work on a Macbook and use most Apple products, so I use GarageBand for all my composition and creation needs. Their mobile version allows me to create and change on the go and when I'm home I can just export the files back to my computer to carry on where I stopped the last time.

- **Instruments**

While having an instrument isn't a necessity, as there are digital versions readily available, I suggest keeping any other instruments with you in your small studio. This will help you in a pinch if you want to recreate a sound or create a new sound but are uncertain what the notation will be.

I personally use the Piano that is a part of the GarageBand software I mentioned previously. It allows me to change settings so I can alter my key signature and my time signature, allowing me to keep track of changes to my composition the entire time I'm working. The software also allows me to export whatever I have worked on to a digital file that I can print my sheet music or use the digital version on my phone whenever I need.

- **Form of Hydration**

Whilst most people will laugh at the idea of having water or something near them while they are working but one of the most important things to remember is that when you get busy with something and it becomes a mentally intensive activity, hydration, especially water will keep you from getting headaches and exhausted too quickly.

I always have a bottle of water and some healthy snacks with me, especially if I know I'm going to be working for more than two hours. It is also important to take breaks now and then. Taking a quick walk around the house to stretch your legs will help you and your process in the long run.

Obviously taking a break while you are busy writing and in the "zone" as they say will only disrupt your workflow, so try and stay as structured as you can when it comes to taking breaks.

- **Trash Can**

While this is a minor necessity, I think having a place to trash all the notes and compositions you are unhappy with is great. If you do not want to trash them, you are more than welcome to keep them in a singular separate place— they may come in handy to refer back to if you need some inspiration or want to make something out of the ordinary.

- **Comfortable Chair**

This goes without saying but having a comfortable chair to sit in will help you and your back. Sitting at your desk, or keyboard for long periods will cause body ache. This is natural, but we can always try to minimize it.

Having a comfortable chair will also help you stay feeling good and cozy for longer periods, making those creative sessions that much more exciting and fun.

5. Organization

The way you organize and make the space as convenient for you as possible will only allow you to produce better results in the end. Adding small things, whether it be furniture or setup to the studio or room you are using will make the process more convenient.

One of the most convenient things I enjoy is a music ledge. Most hardware stores will carry this. A small ledge that can be screwed or stuck to the wall just above your desk, making it easier to access your notes or sheet music. This is extremely convenient as it takes up minimal space and acts as a permanent music stand.

Another great way to organize your space is to have a shelf or small bookcase that is attached to your wall. Keep your floor clear and everything neat on the shelves. This is not a necessity but will help you stay organized and assist the overall positive feeling of being organized and keeping the feng shui clear.

READ ANY COMPOSITION

Now that you know some basic theory and tools, I am going to cover the basics of reading and composition. This will be a short chapter as the process is relatively easy to understand and execute.

This process can be split into four simple steps, most of which are identifying sections of the compositional and then slowly piecing the sections together.

I will include a small section of a composition and use that for the information given in the step-by-step process.

Step 1: Signatures

The first step will be to identify the time signature and the key signature. This will allow you to gauge what the tempo and pulse of the composition will be, as well as the starting point.

The image above does not indicate a tempo (beat per minute, however, we can establish the time signature of 2/4. It also indicated the composition begins with a C Major note.

Step 2: Rests And Rhythms

The next thing you want to look at is places where there might be any rests or repetition that can be found. This will help us establish a base rhythm and pattern for the composition.

In the example we find one repetition, more commonly seen as a loop, meaning that the second bar will be repeated once.

Step 3: Instruments

The third thing you want to identify is any notation regarding instruments. More often than not composers add-in which instruments need to play which stave section of a composition.

Unfortunately in our example, there are not multiple staves. Still, in multi-instrument pieces, composers indicate what type of instrument and how many of that specified instrument needs to be playing that stave.

Step 4: Vocals

The final part will be locating any part that is dedicated to being a vocal stave. These are a little more difficult to find unless the composer included the lyrics with the stave. If they did not include the lyrics you can simply use the stems as an indicator for where the vocal stave will be.

Like with instruments, composers will add a note to the left of the stave to indicate the voice quality they want for a specific stave section or composition. This makes it far easier for you to stay on top of what the piece requires from you.

These four steps are broadly explained and can be used as a guide to slowly learn how to read music. Take your time when you are learning how to read compositions as difficult and busy compositions might confuse you.

Make notes when you start. Use different colored markers to indicate the different parts of a composition; do not be afraid to break each stave up into bars and figure out their notation section by section.

This will take time to get right, which is perfectly fine— if not encouraged! You are still a beginner and being able to do this is not an easy feat.

PART II

MUSIC COMPOSITION THEORY

Section two will cover the cross-over between knowing the basics of music theory and understanding how they work to being able to write your own compositions.

This section will cover the basics that every beginner needs to know, along with the best ways to start composing your music. It also includes the best tips and tricks for beginners. I have also included a chapter where I discuss different resources for those that need alternatives or extra guidance and help. The resources and knowledge provided in this section will assist to make the entire process much easier for yourself.

MUSIC THEORY TO MUSIC COMPOSITION

Moving from the basics of music theory to actual music composition is a very tedious task and will take some time. In this chapter, I will cover the best way to move from reading compositions and finding a workflow for you to starting the process of writing compositions.

What few people seem to understand is that it is not just sitting for an hour and writing down a few notes to successfully have the perfect composition. This is very hard work. Make sure the harmonies blend together, that the tempo is just right to evoke the correct memories and feelings from whoever is listening to the song, notating the composition so any musician can play your piece — this all takes hard work, brainpower, and focus.

Great compositions do not stir the souls of those that hear them because it is easy. Instead, they inspire people to do more with their lives because they stir your soul. Being able to create that comes with a great deal of work and dedication.

It is extremely important to remember that no matter what, you won't always have the energy or time or passion to sit down and do this— that is perfectly fine. As I mentioned before this is quite the task and having added pressure might make the experience unpleasant. Take your time and hone your skills before deep diving into a composition like Mozart's. You do not want to begin feeling bad for not being able to create something as harmonious.

During the process, inspiration might strike and you will immediately want to create the sound and composition in your head but unfortunately, that is not always possible. You need to be able to break the song in your head into parts to identify the pieces that all make a whole. Ear training is something that can come in handy, but this skill will not be enough for you to be able to recreate what you are hearing in your head. Therefore knowing the basics of music theory will help you greatly in this instance.

Remember that music theory is not just what you can learn from a textbook or a single video online. Music theory is understanding basic concepts in the musical genre and knowing how they influence and affect each other— most of the time an explanation one person gives does not make sense and can not provide all the knowledge needed. But do not feel discouraged. There is much to learn; always remember your main goal should be trying to understand the different elements. Once you understand them on an individual level, you can begin piecing them together and begin to see how they influence and change each other. You'll soon become familiar with how to best use these elements together to create the best sounds.

As highlighted in the previous section, there are fundamentals that you need to understand and know how they affect the entire track and composition. In the coming content, I will cover those three fundamentals in depth to allow you a better understanding of what they do and how they affect the entire process.

Melody

Melody can be described as the individual elements that are strung together to create a composition. It is one of the building blocks for a harmonic and successful-sounding composition.

Knowing that melody is created by stringing a multitude of notes with different pitches and duration together will help you under-stand how it impacts the entire composition. It is however important to note that a melody is not just a grouping of random notes, but instead a grouping of notes that are easily identifiable by ear— making them the main focus of any song. Any other sounds that go along with the melody are referred to as embellishments.

Melody will generally create an arch shape on the staves. This is not a must. However, having notes that stay at the same pitch will become boring and might fade into the background. Generally, notes should have pitch changes; having a note jump two or three different pitches will only make the sound harsh, so you can also have the pitch go down in small increments, letting the sound change far more smoothly. The curved shape that can be found within good melodies can be seen when looking at the stave, simply trail your finger along the tops of the notes, starting from left to right. Melody can most commonly be described as rising or arch-shaped.

Melody also has a motion. This seems confusing as the notes are not moving. But remember, within the confines of what the sound makes, the speed at which the melody rises and falls is commonly referred to as the melodic motion. There are commonly two different ways you can identify a melodic motion.

- *Conjunct* melodies are ones where there are minor pitch changes between notes, and the melody generally rises and falls in small increments.
- *Disjunct* melodies are the opposite. They are found where there are big changes in pitch between notes and the melody rises and falls harshly.

The best type of melodies, I have found, are ones that have a healthy balance of both conjunct and disjunct melodies.

Melodies, like normal sentences, have phrases. Musical phrasing is found when a grouping of notes creates an idea or feeling; whilst you can understand the feeling that has been created, the phrase of notes does not encompass the entire melody. The easiest way to understand melodic phrasing and how it is represented in compositions is similar to normal sentences— there are breathing spots, sentence structures, and grammatical rules. Generally, the notes will follow the same structure, letting the singer or player know that there is a small rest, even though it is not indicated in the notation.

Alongside musical phrasing, one can often find motifs. Motifs, like phrasing, are small concepts or ideas, but motifs are even smaller than musical phrases. They have created the exact same way that musical phrases are created, however, they are oftentimes repeated at exactly the same spot in different staves or exactly in the same way, note and pitch-wise. Motifs can also differ in key or the tempo can be slower or faster.

Composers often use *leitmotifs* during stage productions or shows. This can even be found in some films. *Leitmotifs* are found when the same musical phrasing or motif is used every single time a specific actor appears. The motif might sound different depending on the feelings or situation that is being portrayed, but the base musical phrase remains the same.

Melodies can also have counterpoints. Counterpoints are found when there are multiple melodies present. Alongside counterpoints, we find that most composers create themes in their compositions. This means that a certain section of a melody, usually a longer section than just a phrase, is repeated throughout the piece. Themes usually have multiple phrases or one long-phrase. Themes are most commonly found in symphony compositions where multiple themes are commonplace.

Themes are most commonly found in films when a long-phrase is used to link to a specific character. This means that even if the character is not on the screen, playing the phrase will remind you of the character.

Melodies are an amazing way to create truly unique experiences for each individual that listens to a specific song or watches a film and understanding the basis of this will allow you to create even better compositions.

Harmony

Harmony is most commonly found when two different pitches are being played at the same time. Like melody and rhythm, it is one of the base components of a good composition. Differently, though, harmony is very dependent on some of the other elements to create a successful sound.

Harmony will be found whenever two or more note pitches are being played at the same time. What many people assume is that harmony always has to be harmonious, but more often than not it is far more dissonant than it is harmonious.

Western music has one of the most developed conceptions of harmony, and unlike other elements in Western musical culture, harmony is built up of different parts.

Harmonic Textures

Harmonic textures can be split into five different types of textures. Textures add different types of harmonic sound to a composition.

1. Implied harmony

Implied harmony is one of the most interesting textures that can be added to any composition. Implied harmony is found when a melody has been constructed in such a way that it implies the type of harmony that would go along with it, even though there are no notes that are sounding at the same time. These are found when listening to a melody and hearing the harmony in your head, even though no harmonies are playing.

Implied harmony can be found everywhere but is most commonly found in tracks that use the American flute.

2. Drones

Drones are one of the easiest ways to add harmony to your compositions. Drones are notes that very rarely and sometimes never change, no matter where they are being played in the composition. They are most commonly found in bagpipe music.

3. Parallel Harmony

Parallel harmonies are exactly what you think they are. They are harmonies that are found when different lines in the composition rise and/or fall at the same time. This most commonly happens right after the melody is played out.

4. Homophony

Homophony is another basic texture that is quite common. It can be found when there is a melody that stands out enough that the listener knows it's the melody. Everything else is then considered accompaniment and harmony.

5. Polyphony (Counterpoint)

Polyphony or counterpoint is found where there are multiple lines of melody that are all of equal importance in the composition.

Harmonic Chords

Harmonic chords can be split into two different categories. Each is equally important to any composer and their compositions.

1. Chords

Western music and the melodies they contain are built and based on chords. These chords are created by grouping together multiple notes whether they are Major, Minor, or Triads.

Minor and Major chords are far more common than Triads. Triads are most commonly found when three notes are played together to form a melody. More than three notes are often used when they are excluded— creating an implied melodic effect.

These notes could be played at the same time, separately with small overlap or completely separately but at a fast enough pace that it seems like a single chord is being played, thus creating an implied chord.

2. Chord Progression

Chord progression goes hand in hand with any composition. It is found when a musician plays a series of chords in succession to create a specified sound.

Musicians and composers often refer to chord progressions in terms of Major and Minor groupings.

Harmonic Analysis

Harmony can be analyzed and broken down into six different types harmony. The following six are most commonly found in music.

1. Functional Harmony

Functional harmony is most commonly found when each and every chord that is used, serves as a way to enhance and underpin the form of the composition. Functional harmony is common practice in all music; oftentimes you can use drones as a non-functional harmony.

Still, it is best to stick to functional harmonies when beginning.

2. Harmonic Rhythm

Harmonic rhythm indicates the frequency in which chords change. Slow harmonic rhythms indicate that chords rarely change while fast harmonic rhythms show that chords change far more frequently.

It is important to note that harmonic rhythm can be completely separate from any other tempo structures and rhythms in a composition.

3. Cadence

Cadence is most commonly found when the music sounds like it has come to either a permanent or temporary stop. Western music ties cadence and harmony together more often than other music categorizations.

4. Diatonic

Diatonic harmonies are commonly known as harmonies that will stay in a single key. Whether it is minor or major, the key for that specific composition will not change.

5. Chromatic

Chromatic harmonies do not stay in one key— the opposite of Diatonic harmonies. This means that because there are a lot more notes in these harmonies, the keys for these notes often change.

6. Dissonance

Dissonance is most commonly found when a note does not fall into the triadic views of notes. The sound is often referred to as jarring and surprising as it may have a different pitch and key than the others, making it a striking change in the harmony.

Harmonic Accompaniment

Harmonic accompaniment is discussed and explained to be everything that is not the melody. Accompaniment can be split into four different categories.

1. Melodic Line

The melodic line is the string of notes that are considered to be the melody.

2. Bass Line

Bass notes are commonly known to be the lowest of the notes. Knowing this we can state that the bass line would be the grouping or string of notes that are the lowest in an arrangement. Basic physics laws dictate that the bass line is used to set up the harmonic lines that every other part needs to combine with.

Basslines are extremely important for both the harmony and the tuning that goes along with it. Most commonly the bass line will be responsible for outlining the chord progressions, and in turn the key, making it the most noticeable part of any arrangement.

3. Inner Parts (Inner Voice)

The inner parts or the inner voices are often the parts that fill the spaces between the bass line, the harmony, and the melody.

It does not always have to be a voice, as it could be filled by other instrumentals, and vice versa.

4. Descant

While the melody and harmony are important, they may not always fall on the highest line when it comes to composition. Remember one's attention is automatically drawn to higher sounds. Therefore, often when there is a part higher than the melody it would be called the *descant*.

Form

Form is one of the most important basic structures that can be found within the composition.

Each and every soundtrack that has been created can be broken down into smaller sections, and they all follow some set structure or form. While they do not all sound the same, they are created in a simple way to have the same base elements that make a song a song.

While you can notice and understand some forms far easier than others, it is still important to remember that all compositions are created from a form. A simple example would be that you see cats far more than you see jellyfish, so it is much easier to differentiate between dog breeds than it is to differentiate between jellyfish.

Music and compositions are somewhat more complex than most things. While some music lovers may find that they can recognize the forms and structure far easier than others, it is still easier to hear basic, more common, and popular structures than others.

Most Americans will be able to recognize the difference between the chorus and the refrain of a popular song, but may not be able to do so when playing them a song that is East Malaysia. Classical music however is one of the more complex structures to understand, as they are longer and hold far more than just two or three instruments that need to be played.

Enjoying music without understanding the form is of course

perfectly normal, but as a composer, you need to understand the forms and structures that different types of music can take. Being able to do this will help you create better arrangements and identify the types of creations you want to make. Understanding musical form will allow you to create far richer and more interesting compositions.

Descriptions of Form

Being able to take a composition and lay it out before you, slowly breaking it down piece by piece, will not only help you understand how the composition works but will allow you to more thoroughly understand why the composer chose that specific note or range.

There are two schools of thought when it comes to forming descriptions and how they are structured. In this section, I am going to outline each of these two methods and add a small exercise at the end to enable you to understand the process a little easier.

Letter Labels

Using letters to describe the form of any arrangement is the easiest method of the two. No matter how difficult and complex the arrangement may be, using letters will allow you the easiest and fastest method for breaking down the different parts of an arrangement.

The easiest way to do this is by starting with A and moving along the alphabet. If the first part of the arrangement is A, and the second part looks identical to the first, then it will also be labeled A.

If however, the second part is similar to A, but there are small discrepancies you can label it as A' (A Prime), if there is a third variation of the first section it will be labeled A" (A Double Prime).

When you get to the next section that is vastly different from the first section (A) it will be labeled B. If there are variations of B it will be labeled B', or B". The following section that is starkly different from both sections A and B, will then be labeled C, and so forth until you get to the end of the arrangement.

It is important to note that the process will be easier to do when you are familiar with the music and the lyrics. If you are unfamiliar with the specific soundtrack, I would suggest just listening to it a few times. Focus on the sound changes that you can audibly pick up. These will then be different sections. This may take a while to grasp as listening by ear is not always easy. Especially with music genres like Classical and Jazz.

Listening for changes in rhythm and melody will also help you identify the different sections of the track. Take your time with this method. Start with a popular song you know, then work your way to something more difficult.

Familiar Forms

I want to outline some familiar forms before moving on to the exercise.

1. Children's Nursery Rhymes

Children's rhymes are generally short sections that have no major changes in music. This means that the typical nursery rhyme will only have one letter form convention: **A.**

2. Hymns (without refrains)

Hymns will typically have basic melodies, a choir that will add some harmonizing, and an instrument or two that will add complex sounds. While this seems to sound like it would have different parts, the changing isn't vastly different so the letter form convention will look as follows: **A, A', A''.**

3. Pop Songs

Pop songs are far more complex than your nursery rhymes and hymns. They are composed of different instruments and backup singers and the verses change so drastically that it only makes sense that the letter form convention might look something along the lines of: **A, B, A', B, C, B'.**

It is important to note that most pop songs are generally easier to break down because they want the listener to more actively engage rather than just listen.

Exercise 1:

In this exercise I want you to pick your favorite song— if it is something a little busy, or difficult to differentiate then you can swap to something else.

Listen to the song a few times and perhaps consider looking at the lyrics to help you, but once you are comfortable I want you to take the song and break it down into the sections that I have outlined above.

The best way to do this is to print out the lyrics of the song on some paper, and as you are listening to the song make notes on what you think the different parts may be.

There are a few things that you need to look out for during this process.

- Verses - Verses will generally have the same melody as the rest of the song, but their lyrics might differ.
- Refrains - Refrains are the easiest to identify as they carry both the same lyrics and melody.
- Bridge Sections - Bridge sections are most commonly known for only being in a song once or twice, generally replacing a verse. They are known for having a different sound and very often lead into a refrain.
- Instrumentals - These sections are important, purely because they hold no vocals. They are often found at the beginning, ending, and sometimes in the middle of a song, or even between sections. Be sure to note if they have different melodies or harmonies when there are multiple of them.

Exercise 2:

Now that you have finalized the previous exercise you can move on to something a little more complex.

Take the song you used in the previous exercise and print out the lyrics. Mark out which sections are refrains and which are verses.

Once you have done that, go through these sections and look at the phrasing. Split these into sections as you did with the entire track.

Tip: *Most of the time, these will come out to be A A B A. But some outliers do not conform to this standard.*

Naming Forms

Naming forms became a common methodology to classify certain popular forms with musical firm names. It is important to note that certain genres will have a form where most tracks in that genre follow the form.

Common examples of this would be symphonies. A symphony is known to be music that has been written for a large group of instrumentals. Tracks that fall into the symphony genre are known to have a wide variety of instruments and no vocals unless indicated otherwise. People often incorrectly refer to a large group of instrumentalists that are playing classical music as a symphony; they are actually called an orchestra. Symphonies are commonly known to have three or four main sections, known as movements. You will find silence between movements, and each movement will sound different than the one that came before it.

The most important thing to remember when it comes to forms is that they are not a set of rules to be followed. It is simply a method that is used to create something interesting. Feel free to experiment and intentionally change whatever and however, you like. Music is about expression and letting your emotions and feelings show. Doing so on your terms will make the process far more rewarding for you and any future listeners.

Familiar Forms

There are a few more familiar forms when it comes to named forms. I want to outline the most common and prominent ones before giving a small exercise at the end.

1. Through-Composed

This form has a short section that does not have any repetitions. Although you do often find that a short piece might include a minor repeated phrase, which is then considered to be specific to its structure.

2. Strophic

Strophic forms are mainly created from verses. Sometimes a refrain might be included and more often than not there are repeated sections with small differences.

3. Variations

Variation forms are singular sections that are repeated throughout the track. Most of the time the melody and the base structure will stay the same but then the tempo, texture, rhythm, or timbre will change the overall sound of the track.

4. Jazz Standard

While there are different jazz forms the most common form used in jazz is a mix between variations and the strophic form. You will generally find that the A A B A chord progression will be used and repeated throughout the arrangement.

The most common occurrence is that the first and last repetition will include vocals; the vocalists will improvise and create sounds they wish during the other repetitions.

5. Rondo

The rondo form is quite easy to understand but it takes a trained ear to notice and realize the form. The rondo form has a specified section that repeats constantly, but every time it does repeat a new section of music will be added to the repetition.

6. Dance Forms

This specific form will commonly be created by repeated sections that have set numbers of measures used specifically for some dance steps. There are often dance forms that have harmonic progressions, phrases, and structures for specific dances.

7. Binary Forms

Binary forms are always split into two different sections (A and B). Commonly in Western classical music, the first section (A) will be moved from the tonic, using a cadence and a different key, and the second section (B) will be moved back and the end will be a strong tonic.

8. Ternary Forms

These forms are generally in groupings of three, more commonly seen in an A B A form or an A b A' form.

9. Cyclic Forms

Cyclic forms can be split into two different methodologies.

The first will refer to a song cycle where there is a theme and overarching structure that binds everything together.

The second refers to a short section or movement that is repeated constantly.

The second form is far more common because while the single movement repeats over and over other parts of the track will not be repeated. The repetitions also evolve in some instances. These repetitions are quite common in most folk music, but can also be found in forms of classical music.

10. Sonata Forms

The final form that I will be discussing is the Sonata form. Some composers refer to it as the Sonata-allegro or the first-movement form. It became commonly based on the movement in the first section of sonatas.

These movements can be from the quartets all the way through to the symphonies. It is however one of the more complex forms because of the development of melodic themes, the repetition, and the keyframe changes that can be found within the structure. These changes however allow any composer to create unified movements that are longer than normal, that might sound different enough to the listener but won't get repetitive or boring.

Exercise 1:

In this exercise I want you to take your favorite song and try to find the sheet music for it.

While listening to the song, and looking at the sheet music, write variations of the song.

This will help you identify variations that you did not consider for the song.

Exercise 2:

In this exercise I want you to pick 10 songs, and use any of the methods above to create forms for each of the tracks.

You are more than welcome to use different forms for different tracks, or even use a singular form to try and adapt it to the songs you have chosen.

Tip: *Take your time when doing these exercises. I find that if I rush through an exercise like this I sometimes skip or miss a section that could be beneficial to me in the long run.*

BASIC SKILLS

Now that we have the basics under our belt, we can move on to the beginner skills you will need to compose your soundtracks.

This seems extremely daunting; I understand why you feel that way, but hopefully, after this chapter and the exercise I will provide at the end you will be able to start your composing journey.

I will be covering the two most important skills I think any composer should have: ear training and note writing.

Being able to hone these two skills will allow you to create the most magnificent soundtracks.

Ear Training

Most if not all musicians use ear training when they begin. Being able to distinguish between notes just by listening to them is something that will help both you, your composition, and your musical skills.

Ear training is used to teach newer musicians how to pick up on information about notes and chord progression. In this section of the chapter, I want to cover ear training and basic ear training skills to help you along your path.

I am going to include some basic tools and tips on how to start your ear training journey and how to practice and make the musical road easier for you.

The ear training will allow you to be able to have *relative pitch*, allowing you to be able to tell the difference between two notes that are being played. However, relative pitch is somewhat more useless, because of the way that Western music has been created and is perceived.

When you are listening to various notes and you are ear trained, the starting note will not be important— what is important is how the notes are related to each other and what the keynote is. Transposing can be used to change the key of the track— of course, this is a complex and advanced process that needs to be practiced over time to get perfectly right. Most listeners however won't notice that the key of a song has changed unless you play the songs back to back and the change is clearly evident.

This means that more often than not, you do not need to know exactly what note is playing. Instead knowing the relative pitch is good enough. With ear training, composers can usually identify the notes without having to play an instrument to find the notes and chord progressions for that specific track. Ear training is a great skill to have as it allows you to be able to recreate the sound in your head without actually needing to play an instrument or have the notes written out ahead of time.

There are of course different levels of being ear trained; some can play any song by hearing it, whilst not being able to read music. On the other side of the coin, you have people who can pick out any note from a cluster of sounds and they will be able to reproduce the entire track in a different key. Knowing this I suggest focusing on the skills you want to hone and get better at, then practice them until you are happy and content with your skill level. Continue to practice to maintain your well-tuned ear.

Ear Training Skill

There are five different types of ear training that one can do. I will be going over each of these individually and suggesting some tips and tricks, as well as exercises on how to become more proficient in each.

1. Tuning

Tuning is mainly used by musicians as it allows them to tune and adjust their instruments to the desired key range, as well as pick up if notes are not at the right pitch.

When you first start out as a beginner, having a musician that is skilled in the tuning arts will help you out immensely. They will be able to tell you what is wrong with your instrument and how to fix it.

One of the most important things to try and do is to play with other musicians as often as you can. Doing so will help you and them both. Tuning together will allow you to listen to other types of instruments, plus someone might have a skill you do not. The common way to tune for a beginner is at the beginning of a practice session or class, but tuning during and after the session will also help your skill.

Playing while your instrument is out of tune will only hurt your instrument and its parts. Be sure to tune in while you are playing. Playing with an out-of-tune instrument will only keep you from getting better at ear training. However, until you feel comfortable tuning your instrument, ask someone with the necessary skills.

Various instruments have small tricks you can do to tune and play your instrument at the same time. Do not be afraid to spend some time researching and learning those things in and out. Knowing how to accurately tune your instrument quickly will help your ear training immensely.

2. Chords By Ear

When you play any type of instrument that will generally play chord progressions, you have an amazing skill.

One of the most astounding things about being able to play chords by ear is the fact that you do not need to know how to read music and music notation. Being able to play a chord purely by sound allows you to become adept at predicting what the next chord will be.

The easiest way to learn how to do this is to listen to songs you know well and enjoy. Listening to their chord progressions will allow you to more easily identify sounds that are similar in other music— and in turn, let you reproduce that sound. The best way to learn how to do that is to listen to the chord progression, then to change the base note. This will teach you how the base note change affects the entire chord progression process.

Practice makes perfect; learning how to identify chords from songs that you know, but do not know the chords to will help you become more adept at playing chords by ear. If you do know a song's chords, I would suggest playing that specific song in a different key, or consider adding a different string of notes to create a different harmony that still fits the track.

Having someone who understands harmony will allow you to become far more experienced with this skill, as chord progression and harmony really do walk hand in hand, especially in this instance. I suggest looking for lessons, even if these classes are simply for harmony and chord progression.

3. Tunes By Ear

While this is not one of the most important skills to have, as mentioned it does help you in the long run. And can especially support improvisation.

The best practice for this skill is to do so from the beginning. Take songs you know, listen to them, and try to play them right after. If you do make a mistake, check how long it takes you to fall back into playing, and once you feel more comfortable with the technique consider using improvisation as a way to make it seem like the mistake was meant to sound different and unique.

When it comes to playing melodic instruments, this technique can be mastered a little easier by focusing on the note you are playing and checking how long the time is between this note and the next— where the specific key for this track is or where the note is situated in the chord. These three pieces of information are linked and once you become more adept at using this technique you will be able to use this information to better play tunes by ear.

Using the above-mentioned technique may be easier for some than for others— remember, this is perfectly fine. Using the three different parts together or only using one is fine, and if you find that guessing what the next note will be based on only one of these pieces of information works for you then that's perfect too. This skill can only be honed by personal practice.

There are hundreds of different places on the internet that offer exercises like this, but simply taking a piece of music you enjoy, listening to it, and trying to recreate the sound works just as well. You might struggle at first and that is perfectly fine, but as you get better at this or any of the other techniques you will notice that your overall music theory and capacity to write compositions will get better.

4. Improvisation

If you are considering writing compositions or arrangements for non-Western music genres and others, like Jazz and Blues, then being able to improvise is something you need to be aware of— and have the capacity to do, very well I might add.

One of the most important things you need to know to be able to get better at this skill is to know your arpeggios and scales off by heart. Practice them until you are sick and tired, then practice them some more. Those that are masters at this technique can hear a single chord and create an entire track from scratch. They can play the chord and its scales.

Each music genre has different skill sets; if you are looking to focus on one genre for your compositions, I would suggest looking for classes on the specific subject matter as musical teachers in specified genres will open the doors to music theory for *that* genre. This specialty will help you to hone your skills far more confidently.

One other way to improve on this skill, if you do not have the financial or schedule means to take a class, is to listen to the genre often. Take notes on what they do, jot down ideas, and concepts that you find interesting when listening to specific songs. Next, try to recreate those concepts.

Many artists in the jazz community have commented on how their methods of transcribing other artists' songs in their own way have helped them. If you find yourself drawn to a specific artist and their style do not be afraid to find the notes on the instrument you play and try to accurately copy those sounds.

For this example, I am going to assume that you want to write and play Jazz. Find your favorite jazz songs and select the motifs you enjoy the most; practice adding them all together in interesting and coherent ways, but make sure that they are different from what you normally would hear. Doing this over and over will allow you to get better at improvisation as it helps you create music sections where there are none.

As with all the other techniques I am going to suggest finding a music teacher that is confident and focuses purely on the genre you wish to get better in and book a lesson with them. If it is something you wish to pursue, you can join a band or a group. Working with others will help you learn and grow. Someone might know something you don't and vice versa.

5. Interval Recognition

Being able to successfully write down what you hear is one of the most valuable skills that any composer and musicology enthusiast needs to have.

This technique requires you to know your minor and major scales, as well as your intervals. It is also important to understand transposing as some keys are easier to work in; knowing how to transpose those keys will make life far easier for you.

Like with the previous four techniques, practice makes perfect. Being able to practice this over and over will only help you in the long run. The best way to practice this is to start with songs and soundtracks that you know. You must pick a song which notes you do not know, as some knowledge surrounding the notes might make the process seem easy at first and create a false sense of understanding.

Listen to the music while you are busy writing down the notes. Pause and replay sections if you are uncertain of the notes. Work in small sections at a time; if you feel confident you can work in larger sections but for now, do not rush and focus on only the small section. Once you have done this, play and record the notes you have written down, then listen back to it. Does your work sound correct?

It is best to take note of the mistakes you made, as well as the sections where you were correct. Take note of repetitive mistakes and focus on those areas when practicing. Also, focus on how you make the classifications for notes and how you encounter and use them. This will help you pinpoint how best to improve.

People often find it easier to recognize note intervals when they are associating those intervals with a familiar sound. Picking a popular tune and using that as your starting point is perfectly fine; if you believe that method will work for you then use it to your advantage and focus on the small mistakes you are making. It is perfectly okay to make mistakes, even once you become more comfortable.

Note Transposing

Note transposing is used to change the key of a composition or arrangement. When an arrangement is in a major key, it can be transposed to any other major key; arrangements in a minor key can be transposed to any other minor key. You can change an arrangement key from minor to major or vice versa but this would need more than just transposing.

You need to keep in mind that when you transpose an arrangement and the key has changed, the track will now either be lower or higher depending on what the key was changed to.

Transposing is an extremely important knowledge for composers to have; it will take time to master the skill and technique that goes along with it.

In this section, I will cover the basics surrounding transposing, how to do it, when to do it, and what the best possible motivations for it may be.

Why?

There are various reasons why you would want to transpose a song or an arrangement. Most of these reasons will be for ease of use purposes, but of course, those are not the only reasons why someone would want to transpose any arrangement.

Oftentimes the key for an arrangement does not fit well with a vocalist's voice. Changing the key for a specific song or arrangement will allow the vocalist to sing the notes that might be too high or too low in the original key far easier and less off-key— in turn making the entire performance better.

Some instrumentalists will struggle to play a certain arrangement in a key that they aren't comfortable with or their instrument might play this specific arrangement better if it were in a higher key. This is especially true for musicians that play instruments that are strung or bowed. Changing the key will enhance the performance and allow the instrumentalist an easier process of playing.

There are a few *transposing instruments* that need arrangements transposed before they will be able to play certain arrangements. Doing the transposing for instrumentalists that play the French horn or cornet will make the entire playing process easier and more fun.

Sometimes you may not want to transpose an arrangement for any other reason but to improve your own skills or simply try something new— this is perfectly fine, if not encouraged! This process takes a while to do and should be something you do in the beginning purely to master your skill.

Avoidance

Transposing is not always necessary, and other times you can avoid going through the transposing process as it will not be beneficial. Some instruments allow leeway when it comes to key changes. This allows you to let the instrument do the heavy lifting.

Instruments that are considered chordal instruments, like most guitars, can use *capo* to change the key higher, thus not needing you to transpose the key before playing. Other instruments include electric keyboards, which transpose the keys for you when playing. There are programs and software where you can upload the digital file of the arrangement, and it will automatically transpose the file for you. These are not always 100% accurate, so I suggest quickly going over the transposed sheet music once it has been completed.

While the digital method is much faster, you may not always have a digital version of the arrangement. In this instance, I would suggest just doing the transposing by hand on the sheet music.

In the chord name transposing section I will cover why you do not need to transpose arrangements when you are using chordal instruments, like guitars.

How?

The initial transposing process can be split into four steps. This section will cover those steps, so you can learn and practice how to transpose any arrangement for whatever your needs are.

Step 1: Choosing Your Transposition

This step is the most important. Knowing what key you want to change the arrangement to will greatly be influenced by what the reason for transposing is. There are three main reasons why you would transpose, and each of these reasons has a different methodology.

- 1. Transposing for an Instrument

Transposing instruments are usually seen as instruments for which various parts of the arrangement are written in higher or lower keys. Some musicians that are more confident with their instrument will not need to transpose the arrangement beforehand and will be able to transpose as they play or as they are reading the sheet music; those a little less familiar will need to follow the process.

There are a few common instruments that are seen as transposing instruments.

I will list the most common instruments.

- Clarinets
- Trumpets and Cornets
- French Horns
- Baritone and Alto Saxophones
- Tenor and Soprano Saxophones

- 2. Transposing for a Vocalist

When transposing an arrangement for a vocalist, you must take note of their range. Make sure that you are focusing on keeping the lowest and highest notes in their range. Be sure to determine the correct interval for your vocalist. Once that has happened, check the range for your instrumentalist as well, as they may struggle to play in a higher or lower key.

- 3. Transposing for an Easier Key

When you are transposing an arrangement for an easier key, it will be more favorable and pleasurable to play and listen to. Comfort and skill can very quickly show through musical performance; finding the right key for your instrumentalists will greatly help them in creating a unique and wonderful sound.

It is important to note that like vocalists, instrumentalists also have keys that they can best play in. Therefore, be sure that when you are doing the transposing that you consider the key of both the vocalists and the instrumentalists.

Step 2: Using the Correct Key

Now that you have chosen the reason for transposing your piece you need to make sure that you pick and find the correct key to work in. Once you have found the correct key you can start the process.

If you have chosen a selected interval that you want to change, then continue to use that specific interval for the key changes.

The key change process is somewhat circular. I will illustrate this using a diagram.

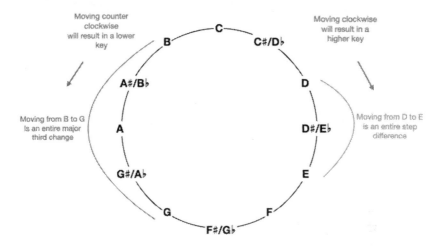

The above image shows the chromatic circle.

It is important to know the intervals and keys off by heart, as well as the new key that has been chosen— otherwise the transposing will not be successful.

Step 3: Moving the Notes to the Correct Intervals

Now that you have finalized the new key and you, the vocalist, and the instrumentalists are happy with the range selection, you can move on to the transposing process.

You will use the lines and spaces on the stave to be able to transpose the arrangement.

It is important to note that if your key signature is correct you do not have to worry about the minor or major intervals as they will be correct.

Example:

The original key is F Major. You want to move the key up by a perfect fourth.

This means that each note will be moved up by four lines and spaces. When moving the notes, remember to count both the lines and the spaces. This will include the line or space where the note is situated on.

This may take a while to do perfectly, so take your time. Practice as much as you can. I suggest doing one bar at a time, instead of working on an entire stave.

Step 4: Taking Care of Your Accidentals

This step is important as accidentals are a little more complicated to transpose than normal notes. Most notes will simply fall into the new key whether they're major, minor, or perfect notes

Accidentals are a little more difficult to transpose. The best way to transpose accidentals is to place them on a line or space closest to where they are, making them a note that would not be considered an accidental. From here you can transpose it by then adding the half note to swap it back into an accidental that has been transposed.

Also remember that if you are transposing an already sharp note to a higher key you need to indicate it as a double sharp, the same stands for flat notes. If the note starts as a flat note and it is lowered then you should indicate that it will be a double flat.

The New Key

The transposing process can only be done once you have selected a new key to transpose your arrangement into. The key you chose is extremely dependent on what you want the sound to be like in the end— as well as those who are working with you on the project, be they vocalists or instrumentalists.

In this section, I will cover the most important info regarding transposing and how the key changes will be affected because of your team.

Vocalists

Often when you are working on new projects you will need to change the key for the vocalist you are working with. This ensures that the song(s) they are performing will be in their vocal range and allow them to perform at their best.

Before simply changing the key, make sure that you are certain about the interval that the vocalist(s) can sing in. They need to be comfortable with the key. As mentioned before, it is important to know whether or not any instrumentalists are also comfortable with the key.

Common examples of when to check the key for vocalists are when you are working with a choir on new hymns. Hymns that are written in soprano parts may need to be transposed as they may be too high for newer or completely untrained vocalists.

It is best to perhaps transpose the hymn from an E flat; by lowering the key with only a minor third you will enable the entire choir to comfortably sing along.

Another example would be an alto vocalist that is working on a project that includes some tracks that fall into the blues genre. Blues are commonly sung by vocalists who fall into the soprano range. By transposing the key from a B flat into an A flat, the alto vocalist will comfortably be able to voice the range without any hiccups.

Instruments

Like with vocalists, it is equally important to check that the instrumentalists you are working with are capable of playing the key and intervals that you want to use for the transposing.

Some instrumentalists might not be capable of playing certain intervals or some might be unable to play them because of the instrument choice.

As mentioned before five different types of instruments would need transposing before being able to play certain soundtracks.

- Clarinets -This instrument is commonly known as a B flat instrument. To be able to get the best from these instrumentalists I suggest transposing all B flat sections a step higher.
- Trumpets and Cornets - Trumpet and Cornet players usually play in either C or B flat, however, I would suggest transposing the B flat sections and transposing them for ease of play and comfortability.
- French Horns - Most commonly French horn sections are usually written in F. Older orchestral pieces will make this difficult, so ensure to transpose any C parts higher by a fifth to make them readable as F.
- Alto and Baritone Saxophones - These two Saxophones are commonly known as E flat instruments. Generally, I would suggest transposing Alto saxophones up by a major sixth, and an octave and major sixth for a Baritone saxophone to make it easier on these instrumentalists.
- Soprano and Tenor Saxophones - Like the above-mentioned saxophones these two are B flat instruments. Make sure to transpose to an octave and a step higher for any tenor saxophones.

When transposing instruments there are four things that you need to keep in mind before and during the process. Just jumping in might leave out some important information, and you may find yourself getting stuck on minor, avoidable issues.

Make sure that when you start you are sure what section(s) and/or parts you are going to be transposing. Make sure that you are aware of how you want to transpose the chosen section and how it will affect both the vocalists and the instrumentalists.

The best way to begin is to find an interval between the two parts you are going to transpose. For example, there is an entire step difference between a C flat and a B flat, but a perfect fifth between an E flat and a B flat.

This might sound silly but be sure that you are transposing in the right direction. Not in terms of the staves going from left to right, but in terms of how the notes will be laid out on the stave. If you want to transpose from a C to a B flat you will be moving upwards with the transposing process.

To make this better understandable I am going to give two examples.

1. B flat to E flat - The difference between the two notes is a perfect fifth. You will then be transposing up by a fifth.
2. B flat to C -The difference between these two notes is one step. You will be transposing an entire part down.

In other words, you will always transpose in the opposite direction of the changed names.

Do not be afraid to refer back to the diagram I used in step 2 discussed in the How? section of transposing.

Playable Keys

Make sure that the transposing you do ensures the piece is both easier for instrumentalists to play and will translate into a better performance. People are more likely to be comfortable with the piece if they do not have to constantly be worrying about playing the right note.

When doing this make sure that the instrumentalists are comfortable with the transposing, as well as the song choice. Some musicians will be more comfortable with certain genres and keys than others.

Sight Transposing

Some musicians have trained and practiced being able to transpose a part of the composition on sight. This means that when they see the note on the sheet music they can automatically transpose it in their head and play the transposed version of the note.

This is the most common among guitarists and vocalists. The best way to make sure that you can do this is to practice as much as you can. Take small sections of a song and start with one bar before moving on to the next. It will of course take longer to master this skill sight transposing skill, but it is well worth the time spent practicing.

Knowing how to do this will also help your composition skills, as this will allow you to make quick changes to arrangements if an artist wants the compositions transposed or an instrumentalist realizes they cannot play a certain key too well.

The best way to practice this skill is to take songs that you are extremely familiar with on a chord and note basis and attempt to play them in a different key. Take note of the mistakes you make; try to work in some improvisation if you can— expand and practice all the skills you have learned thus far. Do not try and change the key two or three steps, instead, try transposing the arrangement by only half a step. The sound might not be too different, and you hopefully might find that you aren't struggling.

Once you feel comfortable enough with the familiar song, try and make a fill step transposing before moving to a different song. Playing an unfamiliar clef will also help you practice this skill. Do not be afraid to offer to play something a little different than what you normally do. This will help both your ear training and your transposing skills.

Chord Name Transposing

There might be some instances where you end up having to transpose entire chords. In this case, it would be better to transpose the chord name, not each individual note. This process is far easier than other methods— even musicians who are unable to read music can do this.

The best method of doing this is to use the chromatic circle I referenced in Step 2. By using this circle you can change both the name of the key and the chord names. This can be done because the chords, notes, and key need to move the transposing step in whatever direction it will be moved in.

How To Chord Transpose

The chord transposing process can be broken down into two broad steps. There are however many variables that you will need to look at in each step.

- Step 1: Choosing Your Transposition

Before you can transpose the chords and all the notes that are in those chords, you need to ask yourself why you are transposing the chords. The reason for transposition will ultimately determine how you do the transposition.

You may find that the main reason for the transposition will be either notes being too high or too low. To use this as the motivation you need to be sure exactly how much lower or higher you need to transpose the new key to continue with the transposition. Again, use the chromatic circle for this. By going clockwise around the circle you can create a higher sound, while going counter-clockwise will create a lower sound.

It is important to note that because it is a circle if you continue to raise the music you will eventually create a lower sound than when you started. The opposite will also be true, if you keep lowering the sound you will start getting higher chords. What makes this method enjoyable is the fact that if a chord key sounds a little off you can change the key only a little more and the entire sound will be completely different, simply by moving closer to a different note.

If however, you are using the transposition process to make the chords easier to play the process will be a little different than the previous one. The simplest way to do this is by changing the final chord to a note that is easier to play.

For example, amongst many guitarists find that the keys G, D, A, E, C, Am, Em, and Dm are far easier to play than others.

The final chord in an arrangement is usually used to name the key. Therefore, changing the final chord will make it easier to transpose the name of the chord.

If this process seems complicated and you do not like the changes it makes I would suggest trying to make the final chord a common chord that is found in more popular music. Whilst you are making this change sure that you are keeping the pitch of the track in mind, as it might lower or raise if you change the chords too much.

You might find yourself in a situation where you need to change the key to work alongside another instrumentalist or another composer who suggests playing in a different key than you are currently using. In this instance, I would suggest using a transposing instrument and moving up the key by the designated half steps until you find a chord you are comfortable with and the other person agrees with.

- Step 2: Changing The Chord Names

Once you have found the reason for transposing, you can move along the process and start your actual transposing.

As mentioned before, you can simply use the chromatic circle to do any transposing. Change only the name of the notes and leave any other information regarding the chords as is.

Do not be afraid to play our new transposition and see how it feels. If it feels weird or sounds strange to you do not be afraid to change or alter the transposition again. Do what works best for you.

In the following section, I will cover an example of what the transposition will look like.

Original Key: G - B ♭ - B ♭ 6 - B ♭M7 - E ♭M7 - E ♭ + - A7 - D/A

2 Keys Higher: A - C - C6 - C M7 - F M7 - F+ - B7 - E/B

MUSIC COMPOSITION

Now that you have all the basics down we can move on to the actual process of composing your own arrangement. In this section, I will take you to step by step through the process of how to compose a basic single stave.

It is important to remember that all the skills that have been mentioned and discussed in this book are beginner-friendly, and most of these techniques are skills that you will need to practice over and over to master.

It is perfectly okay and expected that you may struggle in the beginning. Even though I struggled in the beginning, the best way to get better at the skills is to practice, practice, practice.

The process may seem extremely difficult and tedious to do, but once you get in the swing of things you will be able to write your own compositions in no time. This process is rather straightforward, but there are a few things that you need to keep in mind that will help you along the way.

After outlining the process in this chapter, I will cover all the necessary resources and items you will need to ensure the entire experience is far easier. I will also include some amazing tips and tricks for beginners, as well as more intermediate musicians that are looking at beginning their composition career.

The writing process I follow will be outlined in seven steps. In these steps, I will cover and explain the different methods and items I use to be able to create my basic compositions. This process is rather short; knowing the basics that I have covered in the rest of the book will allow you to make the process far easier to follow.

Step 1: Themes, Motifs, And Planning Concepts

Now that you have learned all the basic skills that every composer needs to know, you can move on to starting the composition process. I always make sure that I have a comfortable setup before I start the process. I ensure I have enough hydration and that my entire setup is clean and organized. Having a clean and organized setup will allow you to be able to work for a little longer. I have found that often when my setup is a little messy that I can get distracted more easily than if my table would be clean. Once you have gathered all your supplies, and you are comfortable enough you can move on to the actual start of the project.

Still, before you can start the composition process, it is important to sit down and take a moment to think about what type of arrangement you want to create. Knowing the type of composing you want to create will help your entire mindset and process. I would suggest getting a notebook and spending some time jotting down some ideas and concepts of what you want to do and accomplish.

Having a composer's mindset will help the entire process be far easier. You have to remember that you are still a beginner; you won't always be able to immediately create the most amazing compositions— that is perfectly fine. You will slowly but surely become familiar and comfortable with the process and with time and practice get better.

The best suggestion I have is to remember that you are only a beginner. Whilst it is easy to criticize yourself early on for not being able to create fantastic arrangements, try and keep your criticisms for later— of course, this won't be the easiest thing to do. Getting down and out on yourself early on will make the process far more difficult. Stay positive, focused, and motivated.

When looking at what type of compositions you want to create, consider looking at different composers. Do some research on how they created their work; look at some of their sheet music and notation. Some of the most amazing compositions are not listened to that much anymore, so look at classic composers, such as Bach and Beethoven. Even though they are the most commonly known composers, their techniques are amazing— sometimes just reading others' compositions will inspire you to create some amazing arrangements yourself.

It is important to take note of the key and time signature you want to use before moving on to the next step. Make sure that you take note of the feeling and emotions you want to convey during your writing phase. Lower pitches generally convey a more somber feeling, whereas higher pitches create feelings of happiness and euphoria. It is important to remember that the volume and tempo also have an impact on how the sound will be created and what emotion you will convey.

Step 2: Base Start

Now that you have figured out what you want the sound to be, you can move on to creating— beginning the process of composing the piece itself. In the writing process, most people will usually start with the melody, while others will start with the harmony. However, I suggest starting with your melody and harmony at the same time.

The best way to get better at composing exactly what you want is to practice repeatedly. This will teach you how to more accurately create any sound and feeling with your arrangement. It is important to work on both your harmony and melody together, so you are sure that the feeling and theme stay the way you desire.

Now pick the time signature, the key signature, and write the first three notes. These notes will indicate your harmony, allowing you to keep track of what your melody will be in the future. The easiest way to track how your melody and harmony are being created is by playing it on an instrument.

Using a keyboard, whether it is digital or not, will allow you to listen to what you have written and get a feel for the sounds of your written notation. The process is different for everyone, so be sure to take your time and to write what you want. If you think the first three notes sound good and you like the harmony, you can then continue your writing process.

Step 3: First Bar

Once you have written the first three notes, continue with writing the rest of the first bar. It seems silly to say this, but the easiest way to get through the process and become familiar with it is to simply write. You can write as much or as little as you want, and then go back and play what you have written on your instrument.

If you like what you have written, decide how you want to continue. Do you want to add a rest? Perhaps you want to repeat the first bar first? Whatever it is you choose to do— write! Writing helps you get comfortable with the process and your skills.

Writing your compositions will become easier and easier; in time you will be able to create pages worth of compositions that you can share with friends and family.

Step 4: First Stave

You have now written the first bar, and perhaps even a second, you have included rests and repetitions, and now you need to finish the rest of your stave.

Having finished the first bar or two will give you a good feel for how you want the stave and arrangement to continue. So make sure you are happy with what you have so far before continuing.

Once you are happy, you can decide how you want to finish the stave. It is important to make as many notes as you can. The more notes you have the easier the recording process will be later. Make sure that you write down when you want cadences to be found or when you want certain sections to be repeated or looped.

Once you have finished your first stave you can move on to the next. Of course, if you choose to stop after your first stave that is also a viable option. Use your writing sessions mindfully. Do not be afraid to experiment with different things.

Step 5: Different Additions

If you want to write more complicated arrangements or you want to challenge yourself you are more than welcome to write something longer.

I suggest that you think of adding another instrument or a vocal arrangement as well. This will help your skills improve, as you will need to make sure that the melody and key stay the same depending on what instrument or vocal you want to add to your arrangement.

Step 6: Transposing

Once you feel confident enough in your skills, you can add more and more instruments and vocals. This will focus on your skills and knowledge, such as balance and tempo.

Remember, that you might need to transpose certain sections of the arrangement for either a certain instrument or a specific type of vocal that you have in mind.

Step 7: Recording

Once you reach this final step, it is important to remember you do not have to record your composition at all. You can opt to have someone else do it for you. However, being the one to record your work will allow you more freedom to make changes along the way.

I generally play my compositions bar by bar; once one stave has been finalized I will play all of those notations together to get a feel for it. Once I am happy with the two staves, I will play them together and make all the alterations that I need to make. You must do this yourself as it will indicate any parts or sections that do not seem to fit or that might be missing something.

Once you are happy with everything you can start the recording process. I would suggest a software like GarageBand to do this. These softwares allow you to record a small section at a time and then move forward to the next one.

Unless you are completely comfortable with what you have written, I would again suggest recording shorter sections at a time. This leaves less space for errors and editing once you have done the recording.

This entire seven-step process is not the only process that can be followed. This is the general workflow that I enjoy utilizing. Do what works best for you and your setup. Everyone has a different way of doing this; what makes composition so amazing is the fact that it is a free creative field where you can create whatever you want without restrictions.

In the next chapter, I will cover all the different resources I would suggest using, such as GarageBand and alternatives for it.

Tips and Tricks

In this section, I want to offer you a few tips and tricks I have come across in my years as a composer. These will cover a wide variety of information that might seem insignificant and minor now, but I have found that most of these tricks have helped me when I am stuck or struggling with a certain section. Often I will struggle with inspiration or certain compositions, and so I refer back to these tips to help me overcome setbacks.

1. Improvise

One of my biggest issues sometimes is the fact that I run out of the will and excitement to write any type of composition— that is perfectly fine. However, not having any sort of motivation to write anything really makes it difficult to even sit down and attempt to push through the fogginess of writer's block.

What I like to do is try and do some practice exercises on my keyboard or even some notation exercises. I also improvise some random notes and quick bars to help myself get out of the slump.

One of the other things I enjoy doing that honestly helps me a great deal is listening to some music. This sounds simple and rather silly, but often when I've found myself without motivation and inspiration for writing something new, I would simply put on one of my favorite albums and play along with it. This would allow me to just relax and not focus on any of my nervousness or writer's block— instead, I focus on enjoying the music.

In turn, being focused on the enjoyment would allow my brain to think of different types of melodies and harmonies for the song I was playing at the moment. This is not foolproof; some days no matter what you do, you just feel defeated and unable to write. I want to emphasize that there is nothing wrong with not being able to write or compose for a few days. It is important to take breaks often. Within the creative process, it is quite easy to fall into a whole of overworking yourself.

This brings me to another trick I would do to help with improvisation and my writer's block. I would often spend some time with a friend who can play a different instrument and play something alongside them. Collaborating like this always helped me feel a little more at ease as they could offer input and different insights into older compositions that I had written.

The final tip I have when it comes to improvisation is practicing your scales. This seems silly, especially for someone who might have some extensive knowledge surrounding composition and instrumental skills. However, practicing your scales, improving your muscle memory, and especially focusing on some uncommon scales will help you think outside the box when it comes to new and interesting compositions.

2. Identify Your Motif for Writing

This seems simple enough, but I have often found that sometimes not knowing what exactly I want from the writing process I am entering into will leave me with a blank sheet that only includes a few notes and some haphazardly written side notes that don't mean anything.

Sitting down and really thinking about the feeling you want to leave your listeners with will help you pin down exactly the theme and motif of what you want to accomplish. Sometimes spending a day or two playing with different phrases and listening to some music that has influenced your decision to create something new will help you flesh out the idea in your head a little more.

This goes hand in hand with the arrangement and notes tips and tricks I want to give. All of these things together will help your process and workflow become far smoother the longer you practice.

3. Arrangement

One of the things I struggled with at the beginning of my composing journey was that the different sections that I was creating for different instruments and vocalists were clumping all together and leaving my sheet music a cluttered mess.

While I understand that some people will be absolutely fine with having notation, notes, and comment sections everywhere on their page, I have found that splitting the sections and keeping my notes separate has helped me better my arrangements in terms of where they need to be.

In turn, being able to skillfully split your arrangements and organize them so that you can keep track of all the different instruments and vocals will help you follow any changes you may make in the future.

Keeping everything arranged and organized will also allow you to write a cleaner and more crisp music notation. Sometimes I do not have time to digitize my sheet music; this can be no good when pitching up at a group session with messy paper. Being unorganized has landed me in a situation where some beginners might get confused or my sections cross and the wrong people end up playing the wrong sections.

4. Notes

Once you have figured out exactly what you want to write and how you want to write it you can finally start the composition process. This is the most exciting part as you finally get to create the creative piece you have been planning.

What I often experienced as a beginner was the fact that I made a note about a new composition somewhere on a notepad and when it came down to me starting the composition process I had lost either the notepad or the note— leaving meme scrambling through my books and head trying to remember what it was that I had thought of.

I started carrying a small notebook with me wherever I went. I began making notes of random sounds and experiences I was having. This was helping me keep track of projects I was working on, and it gave me new inspiration for the new compositions I was working on.

I also started saving images and short videos or recording scenery around my town. Things that made me feel emotions or feelings I had not felt in a while. I even recorded events that were triggering feelings and memories. Referencing and remembering these helped me be as creative as possible when it came to new compositions.

Though I soon realized that just saving these images did not always help— I would often look at an image I had saved and would not be able to recall what I had felt original or when I had saved it. I decided that I needed a digital version of my notebook. I started a digital journal where I could make notes that would be available on all my devices, and I would often record myself explaining a scenario or recording sounds in nature, while in the mall, or anywhere I found interesting.

Having everything digital allowed me to access everything no matter where I was and what I was doing. I found that having access to these things made my entire process and workflow so much more interesting and useful when I did finally get to the creative process.

5. Take Breaks

One of the most annoying issues I had when I first started my composing journey was that I felt like I was burning out quickly. I would often find myself unable to work on a new composition for long before feeling like I couldn't write anything that would make sense.

This is quite common in any creative field. Many agree the best way combat this is to take as many breaks as possible. Make sure that you do not spend 12 hours behind your computer fussing over the same bar of notes. This will only lead to frustration and annoyance.

I have found that by taking a step back from a certain section I might be struggling with always helps me get some fresh or different perspective. Oftentimes I would become tired and stay at my screen, convinced that I would figure it out in the next few minutes if I just stuck with it; but over the years I have found that taking a step back and doing something else like cooking or reading or even taking my dogs for a walk helped me tremendously.

Alongside taking small breaks, I realized that spending days on end only having a few hours of sleep a night did not help me at all. So making sure to get at least six to eight hours of sleep helps. I sometimes struggled to get to sleep when I had been working on a long or big project, and while I felt exhausted I just couldn't even fall asleep. If this does tend to happen to you, I suggest setting up a small routine before bed. Routine has been found to relax and calm down your mind and body. I myself opted for some light reading when I felt particularly tired. I started following a routine of taking a shower to relax my muscles after spending six or seven hours behind my desk, and then I would have a cup of tea or some water while spending the next hour or so reading. This adjusts my mind and body into sleep mode.

You can read whatever you please, however, I suggest something that isn't too complicated or educational as this will only keep your brain zooming. Of course, if you find that you can read something educational before bed then that is perfectly fine. Like I've said before, find the process and workflow that works best for you and your lifestyle.

6. Healthy Living

Healthy living is one of the most important things that any creative person needs to follow. While enough sleep is important, it is equally essential that you exercise and stretch. This seems silly, especially for composers and musicians, but your body is part of your tools and keeping them in good condition is extremely important. Think of your body as another tool you need to look after. You wouldn't let your $15000 guitar get dirty and dusty or let people just bump into it. You are probably going to keep it in a case and make sure it is properly taken care of— so you must do the same for your body.

One of the main ways to live healthily is by having a good diet. This does not mean that you only need to be eating salads and only drink water. Having a balanced diet that includes enough protein and carbs to get you through the day will ultimately help you be a better musician and composer. If you are a vocalist it is extremely important to look after the health of your voice. Whereas being a musician it is important to look after your body that will be performing the motions you need to be able to play your instrument.

Consider adding exercise into your daily routine. If that seems like a lot of effort and your schedule is limited, consider adding a few simple arm and leg stretches into your day at regular times or when you are taking a break and walking away from your desk. It will just push your heart rate up a little and get some more oxygen flowing through your blood— in turn letting you feel a little more refreshed and up to the task at hand.

The final tip I have surrounding a healthy lifestyle is to try and enjoy your composition and musical adventures with people. Spending time with other vocalists, instrumentalists, and composers will broaden your horizon of what is out there and keep you in the loop of new techniques and trends, and will also allow you a healthy break from your creative process when you do decide to spend time together outside of your working times.

7. Share it

Once you have completed all of your work, you may be wondering if it is even good or if anyone would like it. I would suggest first sharing your composition with your supportive friends and family. Also, consider sharing it with other musicians that you have worked with before.

Sharing it with the family will allow you to get the opinion of those that are not specifically musically trained; it will also allow you access to a more general consensus of how well the harmonies and melody flow together. On the other hand, sharing it with other musicians will offer you a deeper insight into what notes seem out of place or what section seems like it was being forced.

Personally, this is and has always been the worst part for me. I am never truly happy with the creations I make and letting other people listen to them leaves a sort of vulnerability that is often scary. Art is an extremely personal thing and putting yourself and your creation out there for people to judge is daunting.

Do not let the fear stop you. Sharing with others will help you to get better at recognizing when there are faults and issues in your compositions, and what people enjoy and gravitate towards.

RESOURCES

In this chapter, I want to cover all the basic resources that you as a beginner might need during your composition process. I will also be referring to additional and alternative resources that might help your journey.

There are millions of resources on the internet that can support and teach you—, whether in the form of extra textbooks, audio guides, or videos, spending some time doing research will help you find the most important resources out there.

Alongside resources, there are some important materials and items you will need. I acknowledge that some of those items are a little more expensive than others, so remember not everything is necessary at first and can be accumulated over time. I want to enable you to use all the resources at your disposal. Using all possible resources will allow you to create the most extraordinary compositions.

Having access to more resources will also allow you to learn techniques and skills that have not been covered in this book. It will allow you to broaden your overall knowledge— making you a better musician, vocalist, and composer.

Reading Resources

In the following section, I am going to suggest extra reading material and resources that will help you along your musical journey. This book along with the others I have written about music will help you along your journey.

I suggest looking at the following texts:

- The Do-Re-Mi of Singing - Aventuras De Viaje
- Mac GarageBand - Aventuras De Viaje (there are two volumes in this series)
- Music Theory: From Beginner to Expert - Nicholas Carter

- Music Theory 101 - Marc Schonburn
- Fundamentals of Musical Composition - Arnold Schoenberg

Each of these books offers you a myriad of resources and information on the topics that have been covered in this book. Feel free to read any of them or look at some online resources.

The internet is an amazing tool— especially in our day and age where you have millions of books and informational sources at your fingertips. If you struggle to understand concepts, do not be afraid to read a different text and see if the explanations and definitions help you understand the subject matter.

Software and Digital Resources

I have mentioned before that there are a variety of software options for those that are looking at using digital software to help their recording and notation. In the following section, I am going to list the software I use, as well as some alternatives.

Recording Software

As stated previously, I mainly use GarageBand for all my recording needs as it allows me to use digital keyboards and pianos for composition purposes. It also includes the handy notation section that allows me to export my notation to a printable format. However I know that not everyone will have access to GarageBand, so I am going to list some of the fantastic alternatives that even a beginner could use.

It is important to note that even though these software programs are beginner-friendly, they do offer abilities that have a learning curve to them. Remember, it is best to try things out and find a product that you are comfortable with.

1. Audacity

Audacity is another amazing program that is far easier to use than GarageBand.

It is an open-source software program that allows you to quickly set up different tracks for different instruments. It is somewhat more usable than GarageBand.

If you do however want to record digital instruments you will need to use additional, different software, as Audacity does not include anything like that.

2. Adobe Audition

The Adobe suite is pretty popular and usable; it is however not a free software to use, like GarageBand or Audacity.

However, the payment is well worth the capacity of the software. It is extremely easy to use and beginner-friendly. All Adobe programs come with short tutorials for basics when you first install the software, making it easier to navigate.

3. Ableton Live

Ableton, like Adobe, is a paid service and very user-specific. I wanted to add this option as it is one of the few recording software programs out there that allows you to record, use notation, and write compositions in the program.

The software specifically caters to musicians, making it one of the better picks.

4. FL Studio

FL Studio is known as a Digital Audio Workstation (DAW)— this means it caters specifically to musicians. With their 18 years of experience, the developing company really does want the best for those that use their software.

It is more expensive than most other products, but if you consider the capacity and output that the product gives it is well worth the price. It is also far more user-friendly than other products and quite a bit better as it gives the best quality output value.

5. Cubase

Cubase is one of the less-known software programs created to help you record and mix your own compositions. It is a little on the expensive side, but the software has a smooth user interface and it allows the user a great quality end result if used to its full capacity.

6. Studio One

Studio One is fantastic for those that want to focus mainly on audio editing and vocals.

While it is a little more expensive than other software products, if you want the focus of your compositions to be vocals I would suggest looking at this software.

7. Reaper

Reaper is considered to be a recording studio at home. It offers you all the capacity and capabilities you need to be able to write, compose, record, and publish any track your heart desires.

There is a bit of a learning curve when it comes to how to use the software, but it is one of the more all-encompassing software products out there. I would definitely suggest this product for anyone who wants to broaden their horizons.

Additionally, if you ever need any support their team is there to assist you with whatever you need!

8. Music Maker

Music Maker is considered to be one of the better audio editing software products out there currently. While it might be more expensive than others, they have a better quality output and allow you more control over your end result.

The software has an amazing developer and the support team is there whenever you need them— making it easy to overcome challenges and issues you may face.

9. Ardour

Ardour is one of the few open-source software programs that has been created by a worldwide collaboration of musicians and recording engineers; specifically designed by creatives to bring you the best possible experience.

It is somewhat more expensive than other softwares of its kind but is definitely worth the money for something that has been created for musicians by musicians.

10. LMMS

LMMS is one of the very few cross-platform software programs out there. It is also one of the easier-to-use platforms currently on the market. Plus, like Audacity and GarageBand, it is free-to-use software.

Notation Software

Being able to digitize your notation and sheet music is absolutely amazing. It gives you the capacity to change your sheet music, while still keeping the original. You will also cut back on physical resources and paper use.

In this section, I will cover some of the basic notation software programs that are currently on the market and give some basic info on why you should use them. Notation software allows you to digitize your sheet music to print it and give it to multiple people. It also allows you ease of use, as you can export your piece to a digital version and use it on the go.

There are so many notation software products currently on the market that it might be difficult to pick. In this curated list, I gathered the best options for both beginners and more intermediate composers and musicians.

I mentioned before that I use GarageBand for my notation as it allows me to export and publish my written notation. What makes GarageBand so amazing to me is the fact that I can play a digital keyboard, record whatever sounds good to me, and use the built-in software capabilities to create the music notation and sheet music for the section I recorded. So if this is something you would like then you can opt to use GarageBand. Though please note that it is only available for Apple products.

1. MuseScore

MuseScore is an open-source and free software program that you can add to any computer without hassle.

The software allows you to upload new scores, to search for scores, and to create your own without hassle.

The software has a bit of a learning curve with some smaller capabilities not being included— still, it is a great product for beginners.

2. Lilypond

Lilypond is one of the most versatile software products to use. Like MuseScore, it is a free software, and some say it is more powerful than its competitors.

The developers created a program that can have additional tools added as the user needs them.

The software however does have a steep learning curve, because of all the interchangeable sections. I do however feel that the product is well worth the time spent learning how to use it.

3. ScoreCloud

This software is wonderful. Unlike some of the others on this list, you can plug in your MIDI keyboard and the software will be able to read the notes you are playing and create sheet music based on that— making it that more powerful.

While the software does transcribe your playing, there are times where the transcription has been inaccurate, and taking time to fix the small mistake is somewhat annoying at times.

4. Dorico

This is one of the few software programs that create quality output in terms of music notation. The designs and overall aesthetic are extremely crisp and clean, making the notation easy to read.

The downfall of this product is the price one has to pay for the quality notation services it offers. The price ranges between $150 to $850, depending on the package you select. If you feel that it is a worthwhile investment then I would suggest looking into it. However, if you are just a beginner, I would suggest opting for a cheaper or free product at the moment and coming back to this resource later.

5. Forte

Forte offers a fantastic user interface, making it easy to use for everyone. There have however been some issues with the graphic charts in the software, so be aware of that.

It is a basic software fit for beginners that fills the needs of what it was made for. The price ranges from $25 to $230 depending on the package you select.

6. Finale

Finale is one of the better software programs out there for those looking into composition and notation. It is fairly basic in terms of user interface, but some rules are created within the software surrounding music.

I would suggest this program to those who are a little more versed in music theory to make the slight learning curve a little less intense.

7. Sibelius

While this software program has a great user interface and notation structure. However, it is common knowledge in the music scene that its real-time performance is absolutely ridiculous and many stray away from it purely because of this reason.

Still, I do feel that the notation capabilities it ensures to offer to redeem the software, especially for beginners.

8. PreSonus Notion

On the more expensive scale, this software offers a great library to choose from when it comes to scoring selection and searching.

The software has a bit of a learning curve but even for beginners is user-friendly.

9. DeluxeNote

DeluxeNote is still in some of its developing phases, but the interface is extremely user-friendly and easily usable for beginners with basic music notation knowledge.

10. Mustud

What makes this software amazing is the fact that it is available on all iOS or MacOS platforms. The software is user-friendly and the learning curve is pretty basic.

This software is super nice for all the beginners that are just getting into music notation.

Remember it is important to try out different softwares and find whatever works the best for you. Each musician and composer has their workflow; it is important to find what you are most comfortable with. Take your time to figure out how you want the workflow to proceed and what you want to do during the creative process. This is something that will take time to do— it is trial and error. So be patient with yourself and make sure that what you do is something you feel comfortable and happy with.

CONCLUSION

When I started writing this book I wanted to share my musical knowledge with both beginners and those more versed in the musical arts. I wanted to create a guide to help anyone to become the best composer they could be.

I included as much information surrounding the basics as I possibly could; since I knew that beginners would need more time and attention devoted to sections touching on basic music theory as well as more advanced techniques, like transposing and improvisation. I also included a basic glossary at the end of the book to help those that are completely new to the musical arts life.

This has been an amazing journey for me; I hope that the information I have given will help you on your journey to becoming a great composer. I hope that this journey will be filled with not only a learning experience but one that you enjoyed as much as I enjoyed writing this amazing guide.

No matter what your skill level is and no matter what musical knowledge you have, you need to remember that no matter what, this journey is *yours*. You can write and compose whatever you want. I love musical artistry because it lends me a freedom that only the arts can. I can create something without boundaries, something that is both magical and powerful— nothing can take that away from me.

This process may have taken you a while, especially if you are new to music and music composition. Beginning anything for the first time is difficult, so congratulate yourself. Remember, the best way to combat that difficulty is to take breaks and do something else! There is no shame in not being able to get something right the first time. Especially something as complicated as music theory and music composition. There are a lot of moving parts— practice will always help you get better!

I hope that my passion for music and the musical arts were portrayed in this final installment of my music collection of guides and that you found everything you are looking for, whether you are a beginner or not. I hope that the magical world of music has found a way deep into your heart and that you are forever in love with the process of writing your own music.

If you have learned anything from this journey, I hope that is the fact that you can do whatever it is you put your mind to. I hope that your musical journey is as fruitful and as amazing as you wish it to be! Thank you for taking the time to read my book. I hope that the learning experience has been nothing, but magical and informative.

My last piece of advice for you is to take your time. Enjoy the journey from beginner to composer. Play around with sounds and instruments and create something you are truly proud of. Even if it takes you six months to do so, make something that you would be proud of showing to everyone in your family. Do not let small mistakes and setbacks keep you from becoming great at something you love.

THANKS FOR READING

Dear reader,

Thank you for reading *The Fundamentals of Music Composition.*

If you enjoyed this book, please leave a review where you bought it. It helps more than most people think.

Don't forget your FREE book chapters!

You will also be among the first to know of FREE review copies, discount offers, bonus content, and more.

Go to:

https://offers.SFNonfictionBooks.com/Free-Chapters

Thanks again for your support.

REFERENCES

Art of Composing. (2016). How to Compose Music - Art of Composing - Learn to Create Music. Art of Composing. https://www.artofcomposing.com/how-to-compose- music-101

Bloomingdale School of Music, & Noordhuis, N. (n.d.). A Beginner's Guide to Composing. Bloomingdale School of Music. Retrieved December 1, 2021, from https:// www.bsmny.org/instrument-discovery/a-beginners-guide-to-composing/

Brantingham, J. (2011a, September 7). How To Compose Music, Part 1: The Composing Mindset. Art of Composing. https://www.artofcomposing.com/how-to-compose-music

Brantingham, J. (2011b, September 9). How to Compose Music, Part 2: The Setup. Art of Composing. https://www.artofcomposing.com/how-to-compose-music-part-two

Brantingham, J. (2011c, September 12). How to Compose Music, Part 3: Melody or Harmony First? Art of Composing. https://www.artofcomposing.com/how-to- compose-music-part-3-melody-or-harmony-first

Brantingham, J. (2011d, October 24). Unlocking the Mysteries of Diatonic Harmony. Art of Composing. https://www.artofcomposing.com/08-diatonic-harmony

Brantingham, J. (2011e, November 7). How to Compose Music, Part 4 - Start Composing Now! Art of Composing. https://www.artofcomposing.com/how-to- compose-music-part-4-start-composing-now

Brantingham, J. (2011f, November 14). How to Compose Music, Part 5 – Simple Musical Form - Art of Composing. Art of Composing. https:// www.artofcomposing.com/how-to-compose-music-part-5-simple-musical-form

Classical-Music. (2020, August 23). The best score-reading apps for classical musicians. Classical Music. https://www.classical-music. com/features/articles/the-best-score-reading-apps-for-classical-musicians/

Dunnett, B. (2011). Making Music Theory Easy: How to Read Music 7 Easy Lessons. Benjamin Dunnett. https://www. musictheoryacademy.com/wp-content/uploads/   2011/08/How-To-Read-Sheet-Music-in-7-Easy-Lessons.pdf

Harnum, J. (2001). Basic music theory : how to read, write, and understand written music (1st ed.). Questions, Ink. Pub.

Harrell, L. (n.d.). How to Read Music: A Guide for the Beginner to Learn How to Read Music. Leon Harrell.

Moy, R. (2021, May 7). How to Compose Music: A Step-by-Step Guide. Skillshare Blog. https://www.skillshare.com/blog/how-to-compose-music-a-step-by-step-guide/

AUTHOR RECOMMENDATIONS

Produce Your Own Sounds with GarageBand

Start making phenomenal sounds right now, because after reading this book, you'll be amazed at all the things you can do.

Get it now.

www.SFNonfictionBooks.com/Garageband-Basics

Teach Yourself to Meditate

Discover your inner peace, because this book has 160+ meditations to choose from.

Get it now.

www.SFNonfictionBooks.com/Meditation-Workbook

ABOUT AVENTURAS

Aventuras has three passions: travel, writing, and self-improvement. She is also blessed (or cursed) with an insatiable thirst for general knowledge.

Combining these things, Miss Viaje spends her time exploring the world and learning. She takes what she discovers and shares it through her books.

www.SFNonfictionBooks.com

amazon.com/author/aventuras

goodreads.com/AventurasDeViaje

facebook.com/AuthorAventuras

instagram.com/AuthorAventuras

Printed in Great Britain
by Amazon

17273849R00072